PLAYING

with

PROFUNDITY

Transforming Your Triggers, Trials,
and Midlife Meltdowns into
Treasured Pieces O' Shit

MARIANNE K. WAGNER

Seshat Press
211 Pauline Drive #513
York, PA 17402
www.seshatpress.com
Send questions to: support@seshatpress.com

Paperback ISBN: 979-8-9996544-3-4
eBook ISBN: 979-8-9996544-4-1
Library of Congress Control Number: 2026900291

Editor and Proofreader: Heather Taylor

Printed in the United States of America

Seshat Press is proud to be a part of the Tree Neutral® program. Tree Neutral offsets the number of trees consumed in the production and printing of this book by taking proactive steps such as planting trees in direct proportion to the number of trees used to print books. To learn more about Tree Neutral, please visit treeneutral.com.

To all who have ever grappled with embracing the gifts they bring.
Set them down for a moment.
Pause. Gaze at them with affection.
Delight in all they have already brought—
to you.

Surrender

Kept wandering right through the darkness
Am I blind or just helplessly lost?
Not trusting the Guide
Nudging deeply inside
No, it's safer to keep bearing my cross

Attached to what I think is my purpose
Are gifts given to be taken away?
When it seems that You leave
How can I believe
In a Presence that claims It will stay

Caught in this web called confusion
Thought my life belonged just to me
But the only real choice
Is when to acknowledge the Voice
That assures me I just need to be

Trust gifted slow transformation
In between were the fight and the flight
Then made a decision to live
Just to love and forgive, and
Inner darkness became outer light

What's left but total surrender?
Was just a dream that said it was mine
But it's all ultimately Yours
The music, the words
Omnipresence simply veiled under time.

Channeled Poetry, November 2003

CONTENTS

CALLING MYSELF

forward

You ask I give you the right words in all situations; I ask that you tune in and listen for them. The reality of what is requires only your acceptance and surrender. As you are experiencing in this moment, tuning into Reality is actually quite easy—but it is a discipline. You can fight until you are ready to surrender. You can exhaust yourself doing it your way. Or you can step into receiving, then bring the gifts you are here to give. The when choice is yours, until you know there is no choice.

— G.O.D. Journals, July 2014

What *is* left but total surrender?

My job is to remember where the trouble starts, and exactly where it needs to end: in my mind.

The voices in my head are insisting otherwise, attempting to lure me back into battle. Giving my power away to distraction is how losing conscious touch with my Inner Council always begins. I don't want resistance to stop me from writing this book, but it's damn well trying. Again.

I know it's time. Well, it's always time, but since there is no time, I have plenty of time, except I seem to be running out of time. Forward, foreword. Perhaps even my inner world of wordy distractions is inviting me to land me back in now.

What sense of disrepair keeps bringing one back to the awareness of despair? Perhaps the desire to find oneself, to be pro-found, is fueled by a chronic sense of feeling lost, but to find an answer, one must wander out of the safety of well-known territory.

It seems honorable to engage in a moment of lip-sync, although familiar lyrics no longer resonate. The inner audience clearly has no interest in hearing yet another rendition of the "I Can't Do This" blues. The one waiting for the karaoke mic is rolling their eyes, while I insist on giving my stay-stuck song one more farewell service.

Hey, at least I'm committed to keep tuning in. My preferred higher frequency station is K-NOW. It stands on the platform of knowing now's moment is here to broadcast love's presence. Yet the static coming from its closest competitor, K-NOT is oddly alluring. Getting knotted up in my annoyance decibels somehow makes me feel heard.

Attuning to K-NOT ties the mind up in loops. K-NOW emits a vibe of, well, *knowing*. The incongruent sound of NOT-NOW is reverberating. All this fine-tuning is throwing me off-key. Refraining from the familiar beat of the doldrums, I'm trying to select a more upbeat frame of mind.

Stuck in the static. But maybe standing still, in acceptance, is key. Okay, *now*. Okay, *not*. All clear, here, for me to hear. All stations, go. What am I attuning to? What am I tuning out? Finding myself wallowing in wearisome worry while timidly wandering into wondering, I wait.

Wait. Finding myself? Did I get lost again? Where was I going? In the midst of another meltdown moment, I breathe. Recommit. Closing my eyes, I listen for the other Voice, the One I've affectionately come to know as my G.O.D., my *Guided Omnipresent Direction*:

Trust. Keep going. In this moment, you can sense Me here with you. Let *that* experience alleviate any concerns. Enjoy, in joy, the joyful side of yourself. Bring it everywhere. Let your inner shift shine through your actions, your way of being, your words. Play. Love. Laugh. Be with the process. There's nothing to fear. Use *every* challenge to remember *I AM* with you.

— *In the Moment G.O.D.*

Wow. Thank You, G.O.D.; I needed that.

Writing this book has been one of the hardest things I've ever done. Noting how frequently I tell myself the "this is the hardest thing I've ever done" story, I hear another voice yammering about control, impatience, intolerance. Who in me is doing the commentary? Who is listening? Anyone in there willing to take responsibility for how hard I'm being on myself?

I'm aware of a wiser self within, speculating possibility. Could my story of introversion be the intro into a new version of myself?

Perhaps acknowledging, "I don't know" *is* my path to freedom. Who in me thinks I could possibly ever know the highest and best outcome for any situation? I'm not privy to all the players: the who, the what, the circumstances that are being, or will be, affected. Gee, maybe it's kind of a relief not to be in charge. At least for a second.

I no longer doubt whether my Guided Omnipresent Direction (G.O.D.) is always present; I just tend to forget. Humbling myself long enough to remember what I don't know (but think I do) while putting into practice what I do know (but think I don't) is, well, humbling.

Listen, just listen. Forgive yourself for the shadings of guilt you are experiencing. Even when you feel disconnected, you're not disconnected from Me. Fear and trying just gets in your way, followed by the "I can't do this" stories. If you aren't careful (that is, full of self-care during your process), those stories will spiral and increase. Yet when you come back, here *I AM* in the midst. All it took was your willingness, your conscious choice to tune back in. Forgive the part of you who judges yourself as distracted, trying oh-so-hard to do it right. Trust, relax, go with the flow. This practice simply lands you back in truth, reminding you to trust that moment-to-moment joyous living is not something to get to—rather, it is a conscious practice.

— *G.O.D. Journals, April 2012*

When we're in that momentary space of inner knowing, the willingness to watch for and welcome in those Divine messages, in whatever form they randomly appear, suddenly reappears. We feel seen and heard by an unmistakable sense of connection, elated at the possibility of being in alignment.

Perhaps we're on a divine mission, albeit one we may never understand. Yet somehow, we do know. We are being asked to join in divine cooperation; to accept that invitation from our Creator, patiently waiting to co-create through us, in the way only we were created to be.

Said another way: Life will always find a way to call us forward.

INTRODUCTION

just call (it) the FPI!

Perhaps confession really *is* good for the soul. Besides, I just can't proceed without telling you the truth. My ego is convinced it should know what it doesn't, so it gets a bit obsessed with doing things *right*.

What's this portion of the book supposed to be called, anyway? Foreword? Preface? Introduction? Thesaurus uses them interchangeably, so no help there! Author protocol is confusing, irritating, and time consuming! But then again, so is the story in my mind, which currently sounds like this:

> *I should know what I'm doing! Like Pinocchio wanting to be a real boy, I must look and sound like a real author. Speaking of author, who's the authority? Should I call the book feds? Oh hell, even if I found their number, I wouldn't know how to articulate such a stupid question. Speaking of stupid, who makes these stupid rules, anyway? Committing to writing this book is going to get me committed! Honest to God, my inner rebel is so over this! Screw it, I'll just do it wrong and go to writers' prison! Whether it's the pen*

7

or the penitentiary I'm bent on escaping, there's a defiant deviant present who is determined to break through these ironic bars. But she's being closely guarded by a frightened jailbird insisting we stay safely stuck on the inside. I'm definitely locked in a battle with a part of me who prefers to remain indefinitely imprisoned. No wonder I'm afraid of finishing a sentence.

I'll just go with the word foreword.

Wait. Fore-word? Hmm. Before the word. Who these words be for, anyway? You? Me? Both? Hey, writing about writing a foreword counts as moving forward, doesn't it? No, I'm going backward! I don't know where the hell I'm going! I'm never going to get there, anyway. And since I don't know where there is, how would I know if I got there?

Better get back to pondering proper preface protocol. Damn it. Once again, my brain is insisting I take every damn word apart. Pre-face. Must be something I have to pre-face before I can even move forward on this foreword business!

Focus is impossible with a boisterous bellower hissing in loud agreement with my hissy fit. "No real author goes through this. If you were really meant to write a book, you wouldn't be up against all this angst, frustration, and unbearable resistance. Your rebel is really revolting, in more ways than one. Clearly, you just aren't ready. Maybe next lifetime."

Wow, hearing my own critical voice stirs up a moment of sadness, regret, and disappointment. Will I give it authority once again, secretly hoping it will excuse me from this calling? Immediately sensing my vulnerability, a patronizing parental voice prattles on with feigned sympathy. Pity, really.

"I'm only trying to help. Please, quit now, before you really embarrass yourself."

The hell with Foreword, Preface, or Introduction.

FPI just stands for *Feeling Permanently Inept*.

Shit, I haven't even gotten to the possibility of pondering using the word *Introduction* yet.

Continued confession mode: I've read through and absorbed (translation: barely skimmed) at least two zillion self-help books. Seeking for an unspecified something outside myself, with the intention to immediately find myself, I'm partial to impatience when it comes to getting *right answers*, or perhaps I'm just painfully self-centered. Just realized, I've never paid any attention to any author's FPI. And I'm damn sure I've never written one.

Somewhere between longing for things to never change and longing for everything to change, you might notice a common commentary: *I don't have time for this shit.* Perhaps cultivating the willingness to accept life's infinite gifts and surprise packages, even those that appear to be wrapped in garbage bags, is part of the bigger plan. What used to work no longer does.

Maybe you, too, have spent decades hiding in endless seek. But then, old bypasses begin passing us by. There's a different message: Something's gotta give. And what if that Something has always been right here, just waiting for our willingness to receive?

So, here goes nothing.

And maybe, just maybe, in our adventure together, we will receive everything.

You did not create your Self, but you do get to create your life. Your journey is one of choosing and homecoming. You are here now, connected, aware, listening, remembering. And, part of your service will be, once again, to forget. This teaches you compassion for the human condition while reminding you to come back to Me. Times of challenge are here as a gift, benefitting all who are ready for shift, to see their experiences in a brighter light. Your collective destiny, a consciousness of Oneness, in Love, has always been with you.

— *G.O.D. Journals, July 2020*

CHAPTER 1

full-frontal backstory

I AM accessible all the time. The question is: Are you? Are you willing to quiet your mind to receive My Guidance? That requires you to release your distractions and defenses. Endlessly getting ready to receive, is, in itself, an unconscious tactic to delay. You can only choose to receive in this present moment. Yes, prepare your mind. Yes, practice. And yes, realize that all the Guidance you ever need has never left the part of your Mind where I reside.

— G.O.D. Journals, May 2019

Bring to mind a life-changing moment. You know, one in which you heard something so profound you couldn't quite decide if it was terrible news or a great relief.

I remember one such day. Familiar feelings of bondage were strangely absent, replaced with a sense of bonding. It was as if I dared to believe I belonged. To what, I had no idea.

Strolling through the park that morning with my sponsor, confidante, and new best friend, perhaps it was the scent and strength of the eucalyptus trees that invoked a sense of safety for my inner child. She instinctively knew where to find places of respite, and how to hide from those harsh voices. A vague memory of losing myself in the neighbor's small grove of eucalyptus played in the back of the mind of my then-twenty-something-year-old self. Returning to a moment of enchantment and innocence, lost in inner silence, I remained oblivious to outer annoyances.

Having recently discovered the twelve-step rooms of recovery, I had found a place where freedom to be oneself was not only welcomed, but encouraged. Talk about respite! From humiliation to humility, the possibility of finding relief from the burden of hiding was staggering.

Like many, my younger self had been taught honesty entailed telling the truth. But somehow, not the whole truth, and nothing but the truth, so help us, God. Cash-register honesty, non-negotiable. Emotional truth, punishable by law. Anything remotely resembling fear, pain, weakness, or sadness, strictly forbidden territory. Only those expressly in charge are allowed to express—and ragefully direct it at their charges.

Survival required interpreting family statutes thusly: Be a stoic statue.

No one ever told me we were each allowed to have our own journey in human experience, even when we choose to take the long way home. Maybe honesty is relative, but not always best defined by relatives. Better found, perhaps, in roomfuls of strangers.

I didn't know those people in the recovery rooms, yet somehow, they knew me. Protected by the rule of anonymity, they were free to be themselves. Sans the sham, humanity. Acceptance. The good, the bad, the ugly. Their anecdotes were robust, relatable, real. They got a kick out of kicking themselves, particularly when humbly kicked upstairs. Their full-frontal openness was a relief; baring one's soul put everyone on level playing ground. Imagine: nothing left to hide, nowhere left to go. Yet trusting another with my own shame story required venturing into the great beyond, somewhere I'd never been.

What do you value? Be honest with yourself. There's no need to gamble with dishonest actions—which will likely result in fear. There is no temporary fix. Rather, choose to consistently invest your energy into That Which Consistently Supports You.

— *G.O.D. Journals, August 2015*

Maybe it was my sponsor's proclivity for profanity that encouraged my stifled self to come hither. Fifteen years my senior, she was like an older, wiser cousin. With sufficient life experience to provide solid guidance but early enough in her own recovery to relate to my resentments, she brought forth the part of me who sincerely felt self-righteous enough to be secretly snarky and just a little bit shitty. Nothing like a little trust and mutual respect, since the targets of our gossipy projections would never be the wiser. After all, we were in recovery.

One of the things I found both admirable and unnerving was her willingness to unashamedly own an ornery disposition, unafraid to say exactly what was on her mind. Fortunately by then, protecting myself from verbal outbursts had become a well-practiced survival tactic, so this well-trained stoic statue could easily appear as a neutral, nonjudgmental witness to brash voices concerned about upsetting life circumstances. A little monstrous and a little mean, perhaps it was her demonstrative demeanor that subconsciously offered an alternative perspective to the terrorized child within, who still habitually prefers to shirk in a chimeric shroud. Perhaps her courageous confrontation of collective human despair was unknowingly underscoring something unfathomable, but unforgettable, in my yet unwritten self.

That morning, she was in one of her moods. Still lost in my own mystical, eucalyptus-scented revery, I remained quiet by her ranting side. Secretly annoyed by her boisterous babbling spoiling my inner experience, as usual, I only pretended to listen, dreamily utilizing the power of my enchanted forest to shield me from the rage of older women.

It must have been her sudden shift in tone, from lamentation to resignation, which jerked me back into unwelcome reality. A disgusted sigh of acquiescence accompanied her declaration.

"But this is my life. It's not a dress rehearsal."

Wait. What did she say?

Survival mode, activated. I know what to do here. When in doubt, fake it, right? Pretend I'd been listening with a compassionate, understanding ear. Baffle with a little bullshit, quickly change the subject. Duck from the bombshell, disconnect from the jolt, and deny I didn't hear what I did, two-score plus a few more years ago. But then again, silence prevails.

I just noticed the word *hear* in *rehearsal*. Imagine a world filled with safe people, who would simply just hear, accept, and relate to our human experiences. Right now, you're hearing—well, *reading*—mine. My carefree strategy prefers procrastination, believing I have endless time to get my shit together. While waiting for real life to begin, I can pretend that somehow, this very moment doesn't count. Being present with unrest isn't exactly restful.

But this is my life. It's not a dress rehearsal.

I AM always here within the mind of peace—quiet, calm, assured, and reassuring. Use this time of observation to ask the Director what your next role shall be—but don't get too attached to the part. Roles will change. That Which provides Guided Omnipresent Direction awaits only your willingness to humbly ask, and act. Remember, not knowing is a place of empowerment, an invitation for instruction to be welcomed.

— *G.O.D. Journals, October 2015*

RISKING RISQUÉ BUSINESS

Perhaps pretending life is a dress rehearsal gives us a false sense of security that we'll never ride in a hearse. I mean, who wants to face their own mortality? Sure, we all know that someday, this somebody will cease to exist. At the risk of being perceived as a busy body, haven't we all committed to an illusory life of busyness, perhaps avoiding more important business at hand?

When it seems life is lacking purpose, we may find ourselves asking, "What, pray tell, is the point?" If we are really asking prayer to tell us, it might be prudent to listen long enough to receive an answer. But if we think we already know or prefer not to accept potential answers—or lack thereof—the practical and tactical survival strategy of prudent pretending holds merit.

Ever feel pissed because good ol' distractions just don't distract like they used to?

Life requires presence, yet many expend a fair share of theirs not being where they are, not feeling what they feel. But at the end of each day, we're all stuck with ourselves. Better said: There's something inside that continues to stick by our side, no matter how lively or languid we've been.

Not only do life's more pressing questions continue to linger, but as we mature, they become mega stressing, insisting we pay attention. Who is the somebody you are here to be? What contributions are you here to make?

Welcome back! Your perceptions and judgments of how it's gone so far are meaningless. You have been noticing your automatic self-criticism. That's not from Me—but you project it onto Me, then avoid Me while trying to figure out your next strategy. Have I not been conveying to you that this way of life is a constant practice? You haven't done anything wrong. You have merely forgotten, and then you remember again.

— *G.O.D. Journals, March 2013*

Being aware of one's avoidance strategies doesn't necessarily keep one from reverting back to them when the unknown is calling one forward. Hell, this morning alone, dishes are done, laundry folded, bills paid. I'm not (yet) desperate enough to start washing windows, although there's a voice inside my head that is totally convinced my concentration would surely increase if I could just see more clearly. How metaphoric. I keep wanting to look outside myself for the work that resides within.

The part of me committed to writing this book keeps making the same tactical error: Listening to infinite innovative intonations of, "But I don't know where to start!"

Sure, I can ask for advice from those who've been where I am. Truth be told, though, I'm terrified they won't give me an answer that isn't, "You just have to start."

Having previously ascertained what they'll say, but still not knowing how to start and therefore not wanting to, maybe I'll just go back to doing something else I also don't *want* to do—but at least I know *how*. Minding my own busyness might mean I'll also have to start minding my own business. I'm an expert at prying, after all. Hey, I could add an A to *prying* and try praying.

Judging from this morning's distractions—which, as you can see, are continuing—at least I know how to tidy. Speaking of tidying, where the hell is Marie Kondo when I need her? Maybe she'll tell me how to organize this never-ending backstory in some sort of coherent, relevant fashion. I suppose being older has its advantages, though, since part of me doesn't really give a shit anymore if people think I am incoherent. It's kind of fun being an eccentric old lady. Sorry, Marie.

Wait—if it's only a part of me who doesn't give a shit what people think, what are the other parts thinking?

You can't really improve who you are. You can, however, improve your awareness of Who You Are. Embracing that awareness fully will require releasing your judgment, leaving only your joy. The incident or experience cannot upset you, only your thoughts about it can. Choose not to give power to your thoughts, rather, choose thoughts that empower you.

— *G.O.D. Journals, July 2015*

ECCENTRIC EXPOSÉ

I'm going to take a risk and speak for those of us who are afraid to speak, including myself.

With most new life experiences, don't we all have a fear of exposure? Afraid of being caught, proving to ourselves—the world—we aren't ready. We have no idea what we are doing, and therefore, we must be complete failures. The trouble is, that's usually where we stop. What's beyond those well-worn stories? How will we know if we don't take the risk of finding out?

Maybe our shared mission is to expose that story as the story we all share. Perhaps the collective is sensing an end to the chapter we've been stuck in, buying into a belief that the cost of admission to fully participate in life is too high. Yet the cost and burden of nonadmittance keeps rising. What if the admittance of our so-called faults, our humanness, is the ticket to inner freedom?

With the support of openness, humor, defenselessness, and compassion, perhaps fearlessness will expose itself. At first, some parts might look a little ugly, but maybe that's because we haven't ever seen them for what they are: a part of the foundation of creation.

Perhaps a delightfully unpredictable version of you is preparing to emerge, establishing its meta role in its metaphorical metamorphosis. More fully aware of itself, it longs to embody its exposé, to show up in its co-creative role, in partnership with its creator.

Risqué, this full-frontal stuff. But isn't the alternative riskier?

Aren't you tired of hiding—from yourself?

Notice the upset, judgment, anger you are choosing toward yourself and others. You think you've somehow failed, aren't enough, or are doing things wrong, which keeps you in a perpetual state of striving, thus obliterating your Essence. But it's the experience of Essence that feeds you—and attracts others—rather than a longing for something you secretly fear you don't have. You have this backward, Child. Your hidden beliefs about yourself, or this idea that you must perform, actually impedes the work I sent you to do.

— *G.O.D. Journals, January 2015*

BACKING INTO THE BACKSTORY

The word *backstory* generally applies to a fictional character. Yet the impermanence of the persona, who lives in a consistent state of interior and exterior flux, could offer some disconcerting evidence that, like it or not, our story of fictionality is a fact of life.

What doesn't change is that you've landed the starring role as the main character in your current storyline. So why not play it to the hilt? There's drama, humor, and excitement available, once we are willing to accept that plots, along with certain body parts, are subject to thickening as we mature.

Mature? Wait—that's no fun! I've done my damnedest to cling to youth while concurrently avoiding reliving my younger self's most cringeworthy moments. Thick-headedness yells, "Look out!" Yet underneath, I hear the calling for a more playful outlook. Ingenious or disingenuous, I'm beginning to wonder if embracing the cringe part of the story is exactly what's needed.

With far too many stories to give credence to conclusions, I see how the battle between the joys and the frustrations of writing were instilled early on. Creative kudos often had to give way to someone else's writing, always *righter* than my own. Critique and correction certainly further muffled my muse, along with the ironclad rule to heed the ominous warning of the all-knowing elders: *Never, ever, write anything down that you wouldn't want someone else to read.*

My highly sensitive nature will never be a fan of feedback. Ugh, perfectionism and endless do-overs. Rereading what I wrote (and loved) yesterday, then hating it (and me) today, leads me to critically conclude (in defense of my defensiveness) the mentality of genius will always be esteemed, but the emotionality of genuineness will surely be reamed. Sacred secrets shalt never be safe with that evil entity known as <shudder> *people.*

I suppose I could be grateful to notice that reading is, quite literally, a part of treading.

Needless to say, required writing assignments threw me into survival mode. Now, in all fairness, this book was probably not a mandatory writing assignment. Still, problematic, or not, I keep coming back to a subtle inner knowing: Guidance has been with me all along. The more I listen with compassion to whatever's driving my distraction and my direction, the more those unconscious rules I created are making themselves known.

Time to break the rules.

There's a part inside that speaks from the Spark of Divinity. It is your God-Self, your Essence. You are beginning to see this all works together. Sharing from a place of naturalness inside makes a difference. As the light of the world, you are co-creating heaven on earth. And because that is true for all, exists in all, your job is to demonstrate it is so.

— *G.O.D. Journals, March 2012*

BACKUP BACKSTORY

When we suppress, backups are inevitable. But once energy starts to flow again, things can get messy. What we've been holding in has to go somewhere.

Funny how challenges bring the gift of knowing when the choice for change is simply no longer a choice. Being open to face desperation creates space for new information. When *the nouns*—you know, the people, places, and things that are *causing* your despair—are keeping you trapped in the neighborhood of victimhood, it might be time to move.

As foreshadowed, in early adulthood, I found a safe haven in the rooms of recovery. There was something those folks had that I wanted. Their stories showed me the benefits found in facing one's shadow sides. Dedicated to honesty, sobriety, and well-being, they seemed to share a willingness to unwittingly, with wit and wistfulness, own their shit, frequently utilizing something they referred to as the *tool of writing*.

Whoa, wait—what was this? Writing out your thoughts, feelings, resentments; your shame, your truth where someone might find it? What did they mean, get it out of your mind, your body, and onto paper? Then share it with someone else? Were they crazy?!

Sure, I admired these people, even trusted some of them. But taking such frightening actions myself was another matter altogether. Besides, receiving not only permission, but firm direction, to honestly face in writing all I was feeling sounded almost too good to be true.

Because I am compulsive, writing became my new addiction. Once started, it was hard to stop, especially upon discovering that, unlike people, paper rants didn't talk back, judge, or challenge me. By God, I must be heard! By God! *By me!* It was as if a neutral, silent witness was always present, saying uh-huh at just the right intervals. The freedom of having no need to censor, explain, or defend myself was, indeed, heavenly.

But tapping into heaven usually entails facing hell. An ambiguous awareness of guilt sneakily snaked around the back of my mind, hissing, "What if sssomeone sssees this ssstuff?" I couldn't bear the thought of anyone finding out how I *really* felt, nor the angst of trying to defend myself if they did. Besides, I really didn't want to hurt anyone or further contribute to human dysfunction. After all, I knew what *that* was like.

Yet with vengeance as my unconscious driver, decades of rage and resentment poured forth. Well-meaning friends often presented me with gorgeous journals, but I rarely used them, since much of my writing was ugly, illegible, and unintelligible. My inner story insisted that exquisite covers, complete with elegant matching pens, remain complete and unencumbered, since pristine pages were meant only for the most profound of poetry and prose.

Almost certainly projection, I discovered a total lack of regard for what I deemed to be "less worthy" writing materials. Pilfering more than my fair share of pen and pad freebies from home and garden shows, with their rip-off entry and parking fees, gave me a sinister sense of revenge, at least getting *something* for my money. My resentful written wrath had to go somewhere, so I took full advantage. Writing sessions frequently concluded in a nonceremonious session of simultaneous tearing and tearing (don't you just love/hate the English language?) a warning that an imminent meltdown was on the way. Despite great respect for ingenious inventions and cheery colors, even my poor, coveted sticky-note pads became fair game as I ripped those screeching scrawls into infinitesimal bits. Nibs got nibbled, pencils chewed, crayons broken. God bless every inky, waxy, papery-thin soul.

Ugh. Hi. My name is Marianne, and I am an abuser of writing instruments.

As I pause for a breather, I offer a moment of sincere amends, hereby declaring gratitude for every inanimate object that gifted its life to my practice of unloading, from head to heart, to hand, to paper, to shredder. The strength and rage that broke them served my breakthrough, creating enough inner space to transmute momentous wreckage into moments of reckoning.

Today, I am grateful to share my story from a perspective of humor and lightness. It isn't always that way, though, since I tend to forget that divine preparation is always in the works.

There is no reason to fight or defend against the energy of love that calls you forward. Would you rather side with the voice of impossibility? What will you have, what will you allow? Instead of arguing about that which you currently see as wrong in your world, practice empowering That Which Empowers You. My Voice, your Guided Omnipresent Direction, are always here for you whenever you choose to receive Them.

— *G.O.D. Journals, August 2015*

CONTEMPT FOR PREEMPT

The excitement of finding, and repurposing, previously unowned energy can dissipate quickly.

Lower mind has a habit of taking more than its fair share of my time, turning me back toward upset far too soon. Granted, allowing the bully to take cuts while I pretend not to notice seems safer than fighting. But a part of me is vaguely aware I am the one granting the bully its power whilst giving my own away. That inner battle might just be the most dangerous of all. Evidently doomed, any attempt to defend what I've deemed as indefensible is, indeed, indefensible.

It's okay; go ahead. Reread that last sentence. I had to.

Blessed be. Perhaps dilemmas are a sign we're reaching a point of know-return—a knowing it's time to return to what we know. Goodness knows, listening to continual commentary of what should and shouldn't be is a waste of time. Self-righteousness used to satisfy us but now leaves us hungry. For what, we aren't sure. When we don't understand what we're craving, compulsive efforts to fill the void only stuff the spirit.

There will be days when we have no idea who we are or what character we are meant to play. Dress rehearsal or not, let the show begin. As we enter that dark inner theater-in-the-round, internal dialogs revolve around the mind, spinning us at an ever-alarming rate. Trapped in our perpetual emotion, it seems impossible to stop—particularly if our overarching overture is a morbid medley comprised mostly of remixed renditions of the reality of mortality.

You notice your head is taking off—then it feels like you lose this Connection. You can't. Just relax into it. Invoke awareness of My Presence, through willingness to get out of the way. You are hearing from the inside out—becoming consciously aware of this Connection. Strengthen the muscle of awareness. Uplift into higher perspective.

— *G.O.D. Journals, October 2012*

GUIDED OMNIPRESENT DIRECTION (G.O.D.) INTERRUPTING

Guidance has a knack for launching us back onto our flight path, ensuring we continue our inner space adventure. Maybe there's something magical about mid-life crisis—the crisis of not-knowing.

Despite having decades of recovery behind me, as well as an ongoing interest in spiritual matters and committed practices, the shift in millennia was a time of intense change. An abundance of spiritual poetry came through, often awakening me in the wee hours. I noticed a common theme of encouraging me to stay faithful in the dark. Decades of pain, resentment, and unresolved hurts came to the surface—perhaps ready to be acknowledged, cleared, and healed in ways I had never considered.

Fast-forward: early morning, December 17, 2011. In the midst of an intense coach-training weekend, I'd been tossing and turning, contemplating the previous evening's homework to identify a personal breakthrough. The phrase *Conscious Interruption* kept appearing in my mind, so I jotted it down in the journal I had placed on the hotel bedstand. Naturally in that moment, I had no clue that random act might have served as a form of surrender. Perhaps I had just entered a whole new realm of training.

I'll spare sharing the six-plus pages of journaling I did that morning. Apparently triggered by the carefrontational nature of the previous evening's training, which is probably an important part of any quality program, let it suffice to say I must have been long overdue for a pen-and-paper purge. Collapsing into self-righteous blaming and complaining, I was convinced I needed to dump my irritation at the very audacity of caring people calling me forward. It was time for a full-on tearing-and-tearing session. Then maybe, just maybe, I could manage to walk back into that training room, looking and sounding like I had my shit together. After all, I didn't want anyone, especially me, to know that I was falling apart.

As I prepared to do what I knew how to do, random disruption appeared in the form of a silent, yet very audible inner direction:

Instead of talking on paper, listen.

What? Conscious Interruption, apparently, was ready to roar into action. Not at all sure of what I was being asked to do, I put pen to paper. To both my annoyance and delight, I immediately became aware of a persistent yet gentle Voice, making Itself known.

Through a sacred channel known as a crappy hotel pen, scribbles began manifesting:

How about you trust and let Me direct you? What if you just stopped right now? [journal indicates I stopped, got some coffee, plugged in my phone, and resumed listening, receiving personal direction concerning self-care, and then . . .] The fact that *I AM* here doesn't change; it's your willingness to listen that does. . . . The fact that *I AM* always here, right now, for your Guidance is what I want you to integrate. . . . You are beginning—and I stress beginning—to understand. I just ask that you practice. Don't leave Me in your journal. Take My Awareness with you.

— *G.O.D. Journals, December 2011*

Whoa. Surprisingly, the tone was not at all authoritarian, but savvy and sensible. My usual inner defenses, commentary, and judgments withdrew from center stage. Even my rebellious inner teen (who preferred to find her own way, thank you very much) courteously attuned to the amiability and mellow wisdom present.

The next morning, I felt guided to try it again. Here, in part, is what came through:

I AM aware of your resistance to writing this morning, and your pondering of what that is reflecting. Ah. Conscious Interruption. The alarm distracted you for a moment, but you made a conscious decision to bring yourself back. Back to the resistance of writing and what that reflects. Resistance to hearing Me because you'd prefer to listen to the voice of ego. Where does that get you? [several more journaling pages; then:] Keep practicing, keep listening. *I AM* ALWAYS here. You are here, right now, only because you said YES.

— *G.O.D. Journals, December 2011*

So listen, I did. And practice. And I began to fall in love.

There needn't be any performance here. You don't have to write down what you hear. The structure of listening, then writing somehow makes it more real for you. But if your pen and journal weren't handy, would that mean I've gone away? Stop trying so hard (everywhere) and simply immerse yourself in what you are truly experiencing. From that place, you can consciously choose what is next for you. My Guidance, your choice. Always.

— *G.O.D. Journals, September 2012*

CHAPTER 2

who is the you?

Who is the you that thinks it controls things? Who
is the you that knows it cannot? Who is the you that
thinks it is thinking? And just who is aware of these
thoughts? Who is the you that asks for assistance?
Who is the you that fights and resists? Who is the
you that loves My persistence? And just who is
aware it exists?

— *G.O.D. Journals, June 2014*

Became the song "Who Is the You?"
mariannewagner.com/who-is-the-you

Maybe you, too, have spent a good part of your lifetime
harboring severe fears of abandonment while running away
from the Source that sent you.

Being gifted with the power to make up our own rules and
timetables, we're given endless, innovative ways to play hide-

and-seek. When Creator calls us forward, perhaps it's only our human propensity to play games that insists Guidance must be the one to find us.

Oh, dear. In direct competition with playful intention, here comes that inner critic, desperately, aggressively, attempting to reassert its authority. Bent on straightening out my thinking, I wonder if its assessment is accurate. Why subject you to the musings in my mind? *Speaking of subject*, it laments, *you have no subject for this chapter. Why waste everyone's time?* It might be right.

But who's doing the talking? The listening? To be sure, most of the time, I'm not sure.

Discerning and observing how much time I expend engaging with—or defending against—the various voices in my mind, muddling in the mist amidst the painful, the entertaining, and the illuminating. At least those aggrieved inner commentators agree in one area: I'm running out of time. What if recommitting to writing this damn book is one of the most important steps I undertake in this lifetime? At least I know that, out of necessity, any steps I choose to take must be undertaken before I meet my undertaker.

I need a new inner project manager. Time for an ad break.

WANTED: Strong, trustworthy Decision Maker who naturally calls forth the Self in everyone. Playfully aware, they encourage authenticity while lovingly accepting current experience. In service to inner alignment, they confidently attune to intuition, to ask for, and receive, divine direction from the Inner Director, then willingly act accordingly. Embracing their part in this divine experiment known as co-creation, they know how to ignite the power found in enlightening up.

Thank goodness, Higher Mind graciously respects my moodiness; patiently waiting for me to creatively play out my latest dramatic scenario, so I can begin listening once again.

Allowing your ego's agenda to distract you is avoidance of Me. Focusing on performance drains and blocks your energy—like a kink in the duct work. Connect, ask, trust, release. The concepts of fear and shame are no longer of service. Be willing to learn, be willing to listen. Be willing to practice. Be willing.

— *G.O.D. Journals, February 2012*

PERSY

Okay, new inner project manager, how about we embrace the idea of replacing judgment with joy? The truth is, thinking in puns, acronyms, rhymes, and metaphors mostly delights me, yet drives me crazy at times. But a love for alliteration doesn't make me illiterate, does it? Who cares if jingles, slogans, and catchy tunes captivate my cranium? Ah, me meandering mind. Noticing the word *mean* embedded in *meandering* reminds me to forgive myself for who I am.

Contextually speaking, this book has been floating around my mind for decades.

But dramatic disparaging dilemmas do derail.

It's not that I didn't want to write. What I didn't want to do was reread what I'd already written. Dithering in dubiosity can certainly keep one dawdling. The very thought of facing decades of diaries, desks, and dashboard sticky-notes left me drenched with dread. Dumbfounded, I had long since decided: No matter what was found, it would be decidedly dumb, doomed to die in the dust. Sure, there were likely some treasures amongst the trash, but digging is a lot of work.

Ever notice yourself trying to make up your mind based on the story your mind is making up? As long as I held *just starting* as impossible, just starting would, indeed, stay impossible.

Practical practice is perpetually impractical, as long as I hold it in my mind as an ungodly task. But persistent inner prodding eventually produces progress—often in unexpected forms. Compassion reigned as I reread that dramatic first draft. Transformation was taking place. I could see my lifelong habit of overexplaining was rooted in an underlying story—an intense fear of being misunderstood, criticized, and judged.

First Chapter. Bravely entitled: "Persy: The Unplanned Introduction to the Introduction." Word count: 10,574. Holy shit. No wonder I'd been avoiding this moment for so long.

Uh-oh. Time to cower. I sense the inner critic waiting in the wings.

Who writes an introduction to an introduction? For God's sake, just delete it! Don't reread it, just start over! Actually, don't even bother, since you'll never finish. Besides, whatever you're yammering about has already been said, and much more eloquently.

I'm not always my most inspiring motivational speaker.

Slimming down a carb-laden word salad is an act of vulnerability. It requires honesty, noticing all the extras I throw in while telling myself they won't count. Feeling a bit nauseous. The maybe-I'll-start-Monday diet mentality is chewing at me. Must be time for lunch.

Wait, wait. Stop. Stay with the discomfort. What's underneath? The ideas of quitting or starting over are equally sickening.

Experience knows where those choices will—and will not—lead. Awareness. That's progress. So, here we go. I give up.

This book will just have to write itself. There's really no question in my mind. It's time.

What is being projected to you at this moment? What are you being guided to bring in for yourself, for others? If it is anything but a form of authentic love, your ego is guiding your thoughts. Allow Me to stream and shine through you, and you will know My Presence. What better gift could you give to Me, to others, and to yourself?

— G.O.D. Journals, July 2012

Isn't every story based on an even older one?

In a nutshell, where I'm convinced this brain hides out part-time, the reader's digestible version of the Persy story boiled down to this: a generic name, meant to anonymously stand for any persona toward whom I wished to publicly rant. At the time, though, I really had no idea of how much excess story crap I habitually carried. You'd think that writing a ten-thousand-plus word introduction to a future book introduction would've been a clue. But no.

By the way, have you heard of that 12-step support group, the one for the loved ones of compulsive writers and talkers? It's called On and On and On Anon.

Unwittingly, with or without that sense of wit, aren't we all just trying to convince ourselves of what we think we know, when in reality, we know nothing? Not only is our own context simply based on private experience, but none amongst us has any idea as to what is going to happen next.

Literally without reason, we let ourselves get upset and riled up based upon a made-up story. Vying for control is just another convenient control tactic; meant to infuse and confuse with a bit of combative energy. We stir up just a wee bit of drama to avoid admitting what we've been avoiding admitting—or have been personally emitting.

Facing our inner selves with authenticity is our key to healing. It takes a certain amount of humility to stop taking ourselves and our situations so seriously. The habit of constantly telling myself that engaging with life's lessons—even with intentional playfulness—is a lot of work, is, in itself, a lot of work. See the dichotomy? Something's out of alignment.

An unplanned benefit to this unplanned experience in experiential, vulnerable writing is that much of my self-righteous anger and resentments have somehow dissolved. Where did they go?

Is release into a piece of literature a literal way to peace? Nah. I can't rightly call this writing literature, can I? Shit, maybe I'm not so peaceful after all. Alas, any pompous plans to protect the guilty—oops, I mean the innocent—have somewhat dissipated.

The perceived negativity you sense has no power over you unless you allow it. Once you buy into it—whether you are joining in directly or judging others for going there—you are in a place of listening to the ego, and therefore, you disconnect from Me. Keep practicing listening, Child. Remember, there is nowhere, no time that *I AM* not, because *I AM*.

— G.O.D. Journals, March 2012

PERPETUAL PERSY PARADE

You might have suspected every Persy is just a projected piece of your self. Uncomfortable, sure. Still, our well-thought-out head trips, hangups, and hankerings deserve to be hearkened. We can always find new ways to make the discomfiting fit. Rather than projecting more shame, blame, and irresponsibility into this shared world of ours, why not privately honor our nonsensical selves by giving triggering personas nonsensical names?

Detachment took the sting out of feeling stung. Once playfulness became a private placeholder, I began to realize every Persy was my personality's personal reality. Interactions with any inner or outer Persy wasn't personal, but instructional. I'll go a step further, and venture to say there's a perpetual parade of predominant Persys who reliably show up in our collective comatose state of consciousness.

Ms. Leading loves to lead a grand procession. Often accompanied by close allies—namely, Ms. Information, Ms. Perception, and Ms. Interpretation—they are all so full of themselves, it's no wonder they must constantly spew their misinterpretations, misperceptions, misinformation, and other misleading stuff. They are convinced they must lead us down familiar routes despite knowing we no longer desire to end up in a dead end.

Famous for an infinite number of infamous disguises, there are countless others, each determined to add their own twist to intertwined, twisted thinking. Exempli gratia, why not take Ms. Taken? While you're at it, notice others in the gang of undependable cohorts, each ironically marching for their independence: Hey, there's Ms. Direction, Ms. Understanding, Ms. Calculation and Ms. Communication! Oh, and did you see Ms. Conception, sadly sitting on the sidelines, silently wishing they had never been born?

I just noticed Ms. Judgment and Ms. Guided busily attempting to convince an innocent inner bystander that the most efficient way to rid oneself of their most undesirable characteristics is to pawn them off onto others.

Ever give unusable junk to a charity because you felt guilty tossing it?

Voices of the past, voices of others, voices of the ego's subpersonalities, voices of survival. It doesn't matter what you call them, they lead you into confusion, thus perpetuating the cycle. The attachment to what is not Me is what keeps you stuck and miserable. To break through misery, and fear, you must leave that realm of thinking behind. It seems frightening only because you don't know what lies beyond it.

— *G.O.D. Journals, January 2012*

Perhaps you've noticed similar characters in your inner and outer worlds. Endless human aspects convincingly lead us astray. There's an undeniable fact that most so-called facts are actually perceptions, which conveniently come complete with an ability to shift.

Forever on the hunt to find yet another clever way to hide insecurity, Persy's propensity toward pretending portrays pretentiousness. Whichever part of the ego is playacting, it's clearly, fearfully faking. Fortunately, light always surrounds the shadow, creating awareness of contrast.

Perhaps our only job is to embrace life's adventure in whatever way it's showing up right now. Imagine the delight we might find in reframing every Persy, place, and thing as a gift, here to transform every outdated belief into meditative relief.

Few amongst us have any idea as to why the hell we are here, yet our subtle callings continue. Why not follow them, instead? When we stop hiding from our authenticity, whatever we've been putting off may no longer seem so off-putting. Here I am, writing out my nonsense; and now, here you are, apparently called to read something that just might make some sense.

Let's put some conscious fun back into the funkier sides of life's profound fundamentals.

When you create your own chaos, you are defending against who you are. Your lower mind doesn't know how to be still, what to do with itself. So, it goes back to what it knows: a little criticism, a little fear, any old distraction to keep it unfocused—and busy. Dear Child, your mind will drive you crazy if you let it. Don't fall into self-judgment, be grateful you noticed. The one who is judging is part of the illusion. Awareness takes your willingness. Be glad, Dear One, be glad. You are learning.

— *G.O.D. Journals, January 2015*

THE NAME GAME

Analytical, creative, or control freaks, perhaps some of us are just wired to constantly rewire things in innovative ways—reconnect that which seems disconnected. With our willingness to tune in, Inner Direction can be quite the matchmaker, finding ways to recreate outdated stories into something delightfully useable.

Understandably, you may have assumed my first name was pronounced, "Mary Ann." In the past, when others forgot— or worse: seemingly refused to remember my name's proper pronunciation—I took it personally. My mind rocked with stories of unimportance, unworthiness, and nonexistence. I was the victim of an unusual name pronunciation—no drama or self-absorption here, or anything.

When we don't know who we are, we look for our identities in the physical, mental, and emotional realms, projecting the responsibility onto someone or something outside ourselves to provide us with the validation we seek.

On a Saturday morning nearly twenty years ago, I was literally at the junction when inspiration struck. Deciding to forego my usual 12-step meeting, I opted to choo-choo-choose a different direction and headed over the railroad tracks toward a nearby church we occasionally attended, having randomly remembered a book study for *A Course in Miracles* met at the same time.

Upon entering the room, I was delighted to see a familiar face. Recognizing him as a youth leader for an event my son had participated in several years earlier, I politely reintroduced myself.

Visibly perplexed, he stared at me intently. Suddenly recalling he, too, was a writer, I intuitively tuned into that "don't bother me, I'm thinking" look, and assumed he was trying to conjure up a memory of either my son or the event. Seemingly oblivious to the fact that I was still standing there, and others were obediently taking their seats around the large rectangular table, he continued pacing around the room while repeatedly whispering the proper pronunciation of my first name.

Um . . . awkward.

As I inwardly contemplated my next move, his jubilant reentry into our one-sided conversation startled me. His face lit up; inner puzzle apparently solved.

Sans snapping his fingers and pointing at my nose (although either gesture would have added an appropriately dramatic touch) he triumphantly announced: "I got it! 'Mar'—meaning 'the sea'—and 'eon'—meaning 'eternity'! Mar-Eon, you see eternity!"

Works for me.

The perfect time to make a conscious decision to stay put is always now. Practice sticking around for a moment instead of immediately exiting an uncomfortable situation. You never know what life-affirming gift you are here to give—or receive.

Observe your circumstances, your current emotional experience, with love and neutrality. This practice is stepping out of your story and stepping into your life. Embrace what is here for you. Resist not.

— *G.O.D. Journals, July 2018*

GET THE MESSAGE: MESS WITH THE MESS

If the stuff you'd rather not deal with keeps magically reappearing, what's the message? "I'm here to help!" professes the Wise Inner Professor. Yet transcending the prideful mind requires passing the Reluctance II Examination.

Which repetitive lessons have been your greatest teachers?

Could your quest for finding something new be the distraction from what's yours to do? Nouns endorsing examination won't obliterate enduring procrastination. And yes, we both know you've been working hard. You can legitimately claim credit for any lovely noun in your life. But we also both know the day will come when those nouns aren't so exciting after all. That babe, bauble, or behavior has become boring. You might even feel a little used, yourself, when you realize whatever you were using seems to have lost its usage. Understandably, nosing around for novelty seems like the next natural step. But away from what?

Throwing thoughts, beliefs, emotions, and experiences into Pandora's box does not rid us of them. Pandy, like a faithful teddy bear, keeps our secrets safe until we decide it's time for their sacred airing. Wherever we've hidden our challenging patterns or heartfelt dreams, the support to help us refresh and revive our inner space faithfully awaits. Reason to celebrate, right?

Oh, wait. Sorry to spoil the surprise party so quickly, but there'll be pesky steps in between. Creating space for manifestation requires clearing. In my experience, the sequence of doing, undoing, and redoing usually makes a bigger mess first. Temporarily. Accepting that disorder is part of the call to order aligns us with Higher Alliance.

Stay aware of any part of you who is determined to remain unaware of unfinished business. Which thoughts and behaviors perpetuate predictable predicaments?

Even scrappiness can serve as a forerunner to happiness. Most patterns must be traced, then cut out, before an updated version of ourselves is recognizable. Since many of us have an inner axe to grind, we might need to face those undercutting inner voices that seem to live for cutting us to shreds. But let's not cut any corners that need to be rounded, nor carve out any more excuses to stay stuck. When someone or something starts sounding a bit snippy or a little too sharp, it's probably grinding away at our self-worth.

The short (cut) version of this *leitmotif* (thank you, thesaurus) is this: The attempt to cut around the discomfort, the disarray, and the lessons inherent in life's learning processes is a choice to ignore the mess — the chaos — that we helped create and that helps to create us.

Maybe our collective work is to playfully explore with whom and with what we are working. What if everyone and everything is a necessary part of our never-ending story? Imagine learning to be present in the joyful discomfort of now. How might life change if we welcomed every character who appeared within both our inner and outer peripheries?

Calls don't stop just because our line is busy. Direct experience directs you back to your perpetual invitation: Accept life's eternal gifts on life's momentary terms.

Be patient with any part of you who feels frightened in unknown territory. It simply doesn't yet know who it will be without its old story. Keep a playful attitude. Let your perceived *nonstarters* become your message: "I cannot *not* start."

After all, you're the one you have been waiting for.

Your challenge is to see the Gift, the Spirit, the Christ-Self everywhere; to hold whatever is in front of you as sacred, as opposed to default perceptions of guilt, irritation, and control. The elevated view of neutrality and flow results in the peace of mind you crave. Detach from the perceptions of this world, all of which will pass away. Instead, focus on what you know to be eternal. I know, you think you don't know how, which is why you are being constantly asked to consciously connect with That Which Does.

— *G.O.D. Journals, March 2013*

CHAPTER 3

alphabet soup

Listen to others. Let their journeys enhance yours. There is no need to make what is theirs yours, nor to use their path to judge your own. I do not need you to be a monk or a nun, yet your contribution is needed. The important thing to remember is to join with My Guidance first, so your gifts can be given when, where, and to whom they will be most useful.

— *G.O.D. Journals, December 2018*

DISEMBARK THE TERMINAL

Ever think of yourself as a bit of a weirdo, a loner, an outlier? Misunderstood by everyone else?

A belief that our case of terminal uniqueness is the most unique case ever gives us a false sense of specialness while concurrently drowning us in tale of woe. In the ego's call to be, shall we say, *distinguished*—its covert quest to be better or worse than others—runs the distinct possibility of discovering our special stories aren't so unique or special after all, damn it.

Self-righteousness isn't wrong. But when it becomes too much work, it'll stop working. Eventually, we tire of terminating our own joy, joylessly concluding "this must be my terminal lot in life." Alas! The endless energy it takes to expend every waking moment protecting our defenses and drama.

Consider the impact you might make if disempowering memories and lifelong challenges were somehow transformed into sacred service. What if part of your anchoring was to discover the purpose of your patterns? Consider inviting them to have a gentle conversation with any part of your persona who harbors a secret desire to remain clueless.

But perhaps this all currently seems unimaginable.

So what? Just expand your imagination, allowing any disbelief to be there too. Merely tolerating life isn't really living. Certainly, your ongoing journey is uniquely yours. But perhaps your life adventure is calling you to forgive any perceived trespasses of the past and to land exactly where you are.

Where has your present port o' call led you? Well, apparently right here, in this moment.

You may be further along than you think.

What feels like starting over is simply confirmation that there is no loss, only a change in form. Part of your human freedom is the opportunity for choice. Would you rather experience infinite joy or infinite mourning and resentment of the past? You cannot do both simultaneously. It doesn't matter which you choose; what matters is that you stay conscious of your process, accompanying mindset, and outcomes. You can let them go at any time, but if you're not yet ready, lovingly let that go too.

— G.O.D. Journals, July 2018

POT-CORN WITH A SIDE OF WORD SALAD

Thank God, even our most embarrassing eras aren't errors either.

Circa 1976. Sans the flies on the wall—and ceiling, due to the dairy across the street—my beachy bachelorette pad was perfect. A spiral staircase royally led the way, greeting me back home into an environment that oddly matched my bleeding-heart persona: Hawaiian Punch–colored cushions strategically strewn across the rattan furniture; bright red, wall-to-wall shag carpeting lazily lounging on the floor. Twin rattan barstools nested themselves neatly underneath the orange Formica countertop, conveniently matching a state-of-the-art, push-button, plug-in orange telephone, also rented. An orange plastic googly-eyed cat clock kept the high watch from the kitchen wall.

Apparently delighting in a mustardy-ketchupy motif (what was I thinking?) I painted, without permission, the bathroom walls a bright yellow; baseboards, a shiny red enamel. Licorice-scented black candles and incense sticks, with the intention of adding ambiance, did little to mask the oft-overpowering stench of skunkweed and, dairy-I-say, bovine neighbors. I truly loved that apartment. It was the one place where I could freely be me, depression and all.

Perhaps my favorite legal drug of choice at the time (and, really, still is) was a deep appreciation for lyricism. Unable to own the vulnerable voice inside me, I opted to conclude that music understood what most people could not. It was as if I sensed creative expression came from a higher realm, as opposed to the judgmental domains of those I saw as having dominion over me and my feelings. Heartfelt libretti gifted me with the illusion of having a true friend—a divine receiver, one with whom it was safe to exchange our most profound thoughts without ever having to say a word. Such moments of deep inner connection supported me in the desire to believe that life must hold great purpose, at least for untroubled souls, unlike me.

In full-frontal fashion, I also loved several not-so-legal ways to self-medicate. Getting stoned and painting ceramics while absorbing others' divine creations was my preferred pastime, supporting me in guiltily avoiding required community college classwork, which, if truth be told—and why not, we've come this far—I had no interest in grasping. Even then, I just couldn't comprehend any good reason to waste time in trying to understand worldly things that my mystical mind suspected were ultimately meaningless. With plenty of time for pot, painting and pondering, I held onto the idea that every mistake could be easily covered, just by letting it dry and painting over it.

One creation in particular, the infamous Zig-Zag Man, hung blatantly on my living room wall, proudly boasting convenient compartments for "Le Stash" and "Le Papers." Sadly, I no longer have him, but I do still have the lamp that looks like a bubble gum machine, which I painted with glow-in-the-dark acrylics while a blacklight glowed in the socket—and a joint glowed in the ashtray.

And then there was Potsy, aptly named after the then-popular *Happy Days* character. Potsy was a young cannabis plant whose life I had illegally created, growing him from a seed. He, too, was showing great promise.

Yeah, here comes trouble.

One day, Z man's Le Stash compartment revealed only pitiful leftovers: seeds, sticks, and stems. But perhaps anguish stimulates innovation. I pondered, somewhat seriously, whether weed seeds, heated in oil, might pop into an edible I could then brilliantly market as pot-corn. But I wasn't brave enough to try it, opting instead to create, shall we say, a trip to the pot-tea. Gathering up all the debris I could find, I steeped the whole mess in a cup of boiling water. Instead of being rewarded with a mellow high, I ended up with a memorable headache. Later that day, long before he was ready, poor old Potsy went up in smoke.

There's always room for self-forgiveness for behaviors in the ancient past. But with no hindsight or high in sight, the signs of addiction were beginning to show themselves. I had no idea how committed I was to my painstaking stake in staying disconnected from my unnamed pain.

But we just don't see what we aren't yet ready to see.

Inspiration reminds you of the Spirit within. Things I put in your path—a piece of music, a book excerpt, a divine message—are all there to remind you of the Truth of Who you are. *I AM* here. Now. Always.

— *G.O.D. Journals, September 2014*

DESTINED FOR PRE-DESTINATION

Perish the thought or cherish it; honor your retro. Retrospective from revered perspective allows you to respect the magnitude of your more momentous moments. Stories store significance. Acknowledging them raises awareness; appreciation for the Guidance that always is.

For many, late teens are a time of great contemplation of an unimaginable future. I frequently found myself pondering matters of a spiritual nature while concurrently fearing those thoughts might be better left to someone I likewise feared knew better than I. Yet nearly every time I allowed myself to get roped into one of those uncomfortable religious talks with a well-meaning person, I'd leave the conversation feeling attacked, confused, resentful, and irritated. Defending myself against the demand to declare myself unworthy of the love of God, was, for the love of God, somehow incongruent with the loving God I longed to envision.

Could it be that people who are convinced they must work very hard to convince others that their way is the only way, are actually trying to convince themselves of something they, too, don't quite believe? It grieves me to think that all unrest comes from a deep sense of unworthiness; of being unable to rest in peace while we are still alive. Could there be a fundamental misunderstanding, considering the love we all are?

But I'm getting ahead of myself.

At nineteen, trying to figure out how the hell I was going to get to heaven while trying to trust an entity that apparently thought I was a piece of crap, well, it was all just too damn complicated. The pressure others put on me to answer unanswerable questions, but only with the answers they insisted I must give, provoked my inner rebel, who was not yet ready to make any changes to the unhealthy choices she was currently making.

Yet step by step, story by story, Guidance finds a way, in a way that works.

Stop making it so difficult, Child. You need only know now. There's no reason to have the big picture, for you cannot see it all at once. Your job is to be humble. Ask, then act upon, that which brings you peace in this moment. You are so accustomed to guilt, the peace you seek seems almost sacrificial, as if you had to give up who you think you are. Release your inner judgment and battle. Receive and experience the peace that rests beyond.

— *G.O.D. Journals, July 2017*

A half-century has passed, yet the lasting visual of exactly who was sitting where on that iconic interior island of red and black rattan affirms something epic occurred that afternoon. The friends who randomly stopped by were much older, possibly even nearing the ripe old age of twenty-five.

Unlike chatting with my pals from high school or my new party peers, with these particular friends I had come to expect conversations of a more contemplative nature. You know, more mature, higher quality. They were also reliable in their willingness to share their stash. You know, higher quality. More mature.

Our philosophical ponderings permeated profound possibility, perhaps awakening the desire for divine discussion. This was in sharp contrast to my inner Ms. Information, who preferred to know it all so she could avoid such topics altogether.

Perhaps it was their energy that held the space for contemplation versus an obvious—or oblivious—agenda of a particular outcome. No coercion, just conversation. This day was no different, except maybe we were just a tiny bit more wasted than usual. I felt a sense of anxious tension entering my body as I tried to push away a question randomly floating around my mind. The high moment was nigh. Here, present with my trusted elders, was my chance. So, I took a deep risk followed by a deep breath. "Do you believe in pre-destination?"

Not at all sure of what I was asking, let alone what I hoped to hear, their affirmative answer left me feeling elated, intrigued, energized, relieved, and reassured. Maybe there *was* a plan for my life. Maybe there *wasn't* anything to fear, nothing to figure out, nor worry about. All I'd ever need, I'd have. Expansion, aliveness, excitement coursed through my body. Mind you, this all happened at least five years *before* I was forced to consider whether this was my life, or just a dress rehearsal. But in that moment, I knew there must be purpose, meaning, and divine direction in everything. I was aware of awareness. Cosmic.

Yet in an instant, *knowing* turned into *grasping* — for something I didn't know how to hold.

In a frantic search to find a way to keep the conversation going with my fellow inspectors of introspection, I desperately tried to gather thoughts about thoughts I didn't know I had. It was as if I were watching words in a whirlpool, slippery speculations swimming by before they sank, forever evaporating in a steam of brothy brain fog. Collapsing back into a familiar daze of confusion and mirth, I simply could not articulate anything coherent, other than my absolute visual truth in that moment.

"My head feels like alphabet soup." And we laughed hysterically.

Nothing like an epic chortle or argument to perturb profundity. Dismissing what we intuitively know though perhaps are unable to articulate is one way to temporarily ignore the inevitable. We all deal with discomfort in the best ways we know how, and in those days, we just did what we always did: rolled another doobie and spaced back into never-never-forever-land.

Spacin'

Not sure if I'm of this world
Or in another land
Is this the place to walk in truth
Or simply take a stand

Does it really matter
If I stay or if I go
Sometimes I'm
Just sure I'm high
Though masses seem so low

Secretly I'm grinning
At thoughts to make me cry
Can't tell if I've been blinded
Or just confirmed my inner-eye

Exhaustion appears as restful
Energy makes time to sleep
Observing some are drowning
'Cause shallow ain't so deep

No need to fear these fearless thoughts
Overwhelmed by inner crowd
Minuscule within magnificence
Where silence rules so loud

52

Lost within this tiny world
Though never quite alone
Deep inside
This mind of mine
Something's guiding me back Home

Spacin' in this place of rhyme
Often wonder where I go
But since there is
No such thing as time
Why even need to know?

Channeled Poetry, August 2005

Curiosity was piqued once again when a cheesy documentary, *Beyond and Back*, was released in 1978. Unexamined enigmas both attracted and unnerved me, since I feared talking about what I was dying to. Ideas concerning reincarnation and near-death experiences were no exception.

Upon recent review of the movie's original trailer, the first thing that struck me as frightening were our 1970s fashion choices. But perhaps more importantly, it occurred to me that never-before-considered concepts were becoming more mainstream, expanding possibilities not only in my mind, but in the collective's as well.

My nebulous attraction to matters of a spiritual nature persisted. Songs of the era kept me dancing between the co-misery of commiserating with codependency and the dawning of the Age of Aquarius. Not having for-sure answers stick around kept me stuck. Deciding I would never understand anything kept me mired in conviction I'd always be misunderstood.

Despite my growing awareness of random coincidences and convergences, I chose to focus, quite literally, on smoke and mirrors. Blaming odd synchronicities on being buzzed most of the time, I continued soaking in my own private hot tub of alphabet soup.

Go with the flow. This is part of your curriculum. There is no other information you need. Information, planning, and details just clutter your mind.

— *G.O.D. Journals, May 2012*

ALPHABET SOUP AND WORD SALAD SIDEBAR

Uncanny. There's uncertainty stirring around in my soup pot of memories.

While I ponder alphabet soup, a vision of a much younger me frantically searching becomes present. I watch her attempt to capture on a soup spoon randomly scattered macaroni letters that frustratingly keep floating away. Efforts to spell her ridiculously long name, or at least a rebellious swear word, go unmet. That tastes-like-a-can brothy concoction is bringing up resentment, yet there's something unreasonable about holding a soupy grudge for a half century. What's up?

Channeling a 1960s parental mindset, I can see how alphabet soup was considered a quick and healthy dinner. It was traditionally served every Halloween at our home, with a side of raw carrots intended, I'm sure, to calorically cancel out any forthcoming treats.

My inner kid, however, felt punished. She was getting a deal as raw as those carrots. Knowing she'd be singled out, forbidden to enjoy most of the treats she'd collect later that evening, her annual trick was to look for innovative ways to hide from those dreaded others.

Decades of defending against prying eyes has apparently resulted in relentless resentment. When the horn of plenty blares, high alert still flares. As long as cornucopias stay stuffed with guilt, the battle of the bulge will be mine to lose. Bon appétit!

But maybe chronic body shame has offered valuable feedback all along. Refusing to be a chief enabler — or, for that matter, even a sous-chef — perhaps this body's ongoing challenges are here to draw attention to an unrequited craving for fruitless loops. It's time to grant the body permission to release any function that rightfully belongs to the heart, mind, or spirit.

Regardless, it seems canned alphabet soup, in the uncanniness of my mind, may forever be confusingly connected to contradicting consummations.

Oh, wait—or was that consommé? Still waiting for clarity.

The ability to change your mind is always within you.
Your only job is only to be aware in this now moment.
— *G.O.D. Journals, September 2014*

KNOCK IT OFF – IT'S T-TIME

It requires courage to step into unfamiliar territory. Despite ongoing resistance, when the time comes to accept new direction, you'll know. Perhaps awareness has been on the way for some time, but if was in a form you didn't like, you may have refused to give it credence.

Since it's been nearly five decades, I no longer remember the dramatic details that prompted my desperation that day. Still pie-eyed and high most of the time, life circumstances had become more complicated. I needed help—someone to whom I could authentically voice my pain, my fears. I had not yet been introduced to the 12-step rooms of recovery, so did what any God-fearing person might do. I called a church hotline.

Shortly after I made that call, I began receiving random inspirational booklets in the mail. Still very triggered by the shame-based ideals found in mainstream religion, I mostly ignored them. But as fate would have it, there was a particular pamphlet that made its way into my periphery, containing the works of Norman Vincent Peale. There was something innocuously nurturing about presenting spiritual principles in a practical way that a-peale-d to my inner skeptic. One such suggestion was accompanied by a powerful visual that delighted the part of me who really didn't want to admit how much pent-up anger she carried.

"Knock the 'T' off of can't!" he proposed. Picturing myself wielding a bat while Norm cheered on my sluggish ego, I knocked the crap out of that damn T, scoring the first home run of my pathetically nonathletic life.

Swinging around some newfound energy need not end there. No, siree! Let's replace challenging circumstances with creative thought and kick off another canning season with some more wordplay. Can we kick the T right off of "there" and land right here? You bet we can! And now, let's wipe the W right off of "where" and, woohoo, we're still here!

Instead of going nowhere you experience purpose by being now-here. NOW is the opportunity to develop deeper trust while experiencing upliftment. The more you practice embracing this Knowledge, the more integrated you become. Living in integrity, you naturally teach what you are being shown. Light the way for others, as they light the way for you. Delight in finding the way that is uniquely yours, so you can in-joy your journey!

— *G.O.D. Journals, July 2020*

WHAT A DIFFERENCE A SPACE MAKES

Space changes everything.

Perhaps space is best utilized to interrupt our interpretations. It only takes a split second of humility to ask for the gift of transcendence. Current thoughts and ways of being are a gateway into greater awareness, if we stop and acknowledge that which only seemed to be in our way.

Give space the space to do what it does best.

Pause. Pay attention to all of your cosmic journey.

Notice the next time you catch yourself wistfully declaring: *I'm getting there,* or, perhaps with an air of self-disgust: *I'm just not there yet,* and offer yourself a soothing, compassionate reminder. *There, there, Dear One; don't worry, because there's no there-there. We're only facing reality here.* Alternatively, use the moment to convert *no there* into *not here.* Next, knock the T off of *there-there,* landing right back into *here-here.*

Here, here, and hip hip hooray! There's always something to cheer for, right?

There's only a breath between thoughts and emotions and the meanings we assign them, a tiny space between letters, between words. According to current conceptional compartmentalization, the chosen space allotment in your mind, are you feeling *apart from* or *a part of* your desired alignment? Creating infinitesimal pauses between illations can be elating. Is your power going where you want it to go?

When you notice yourself getting caught up in a fight against yourself, you've already won. Inner incongruence is wonderful feedback. If you've joined in the ruckus of righteousness, criticism, and judgment, justifying ego's craving to feel *a part of*—congratulations! The prize is in noticing there's a part of you who feels apart and, therefore, out of alignment.

How about a warm broth float while we play with transformation? Invite this moment's seasoning to uplift you. What possibilities will be revealed as you envision your inner space adventure? Allow all the thoughts, emotions, words, body sensations—whatever is drifting around your imagination—to surface. Request their random rearrangement. How does the picture change? Keep in mind, you need only choose to move around the letters of the word *reaction* for it to become your new *creation*.

Invite your spacey self to space out. When you forget what you're doing, that's a perfect time to stop and ask: *Wait, where was I going?* Ah, nowhere, you say? Great! Now, change your space signal! Discover what part of you receives comfort by spacing out—or, perhaps, longs to be joined back together. Just like that, *nowhere* brings you back, *now here*, once again.

Our aptitudes and abilities—most importantly, perhaps those we previously labeled as *disabilities*—hold within them infinite possibility. We can instruct our interpretations and interruptions to serve in any way we wish. Ah, instruction. Inner structure. We possess everything we need to co-create new chapters, leading the way for ourselves and future generations.

Your quirks play an important role in the unique genius you bring. Of course, you are different. Creator created you that way. Your particular form of divine expression, however it manifests for you, is your gift to receive, to delight in, and gift to others.

Discover the space between your thoughts. Be a part of. Bring your unique puzzle piece. Imagine joining together in a shared vision that we don't yet fully see, expanding our energy in the present while playfully making peace with the past.

Stay in conscious partnership with who you truly aspire to be—who you truly already are. Whatever space you're in holds value because you're in it.

Time is your life currency. How will you spend it today?

How can you be afraid, knowing *I AM* a part of you? *I AM* whole, all encompassing; therefore, holiness is a part of you. You are a part of, not apart from. Notice how a simple space creates new perception. When you are tuned in, you are clear *I AM* available as your Guidance, it is apparent we cannot be apart. Apparent—a parent. Abandonment only seems apparent when you have allowed parental voices of fear to become louder than My Voice of Love. Your fear of abandonment is a fantasy. You cannot be abandoned. In My perfect world, a healthy parent is always available.

— *G.O.D. Journals, September 2014*

CHAPTER 4

abc fun-da-mentals

Today is a day of great possibility. Your presence is needed. You cannot turn back time, for time does not exist. You can, however, re-write the perceived past by connecting with Me in the present. Although a part of you is resistant, awareness transcends it. Despite the temptation to connect with Me only in certain situations while judging the rest, keep turning back to Me. It's only ego's interpretations of past events that hold you back.

— *G.O.D. Journals, October 2014*

PROGRESS REPORT

Vigilantly, vaguely aware of the vigilante voices competing in the head.

Observe them, hear them, but don't let them lead.
Watch words move from mind, to fingers, to keyboard, to screen.
Judge. Erase. Forgive. Judge again for wasting time.
Voices not quite quiet, not quite quit.
Sit quietly; question. Was that "ahh, quit" or "acquit"?
Conveniently remembering: "listen" is "silent" rearranged.
Must be time to tune in to Wiser Counsel.
A moment of lucidity brightens.
Review objectives. Resetting. Letting.
Wait. Maybe that was objections?

Besetting, regretting, forgetting. And so it goes. Resetting again. Perhaps even discordance, distraction, and discouragement are here for our learning. Provocation, divine invitation. Reactions, destined as creations. Loving intwined in evolving. Reminders that every free spirit is destined to become what it is. Free. Spirit.

With Guidance as the guide, the message is:

Increase the ability to sense sensibility in all senses.

Encouraged to explore, what will be discovered in being, even in denial?

Transformation and edification require participation. Here we are, plunked right smack-dab into this perpetual celestial classroom, one from which we may never quite graduate. Might as well enjoy meeting our most attractive classmates. Whoever we've attracted thus far can't be mere coincidence, can it?

Keeping in mind each member of this human class is concurrently both student and teacher, consider each reflective classmate and collective lessons. All a part, even when falling apart. In the midst of repeating challenging courses, it's tempting to resist reverting to student status, especially when we've previously promised ourselves that we'd never have to learn this lesson again.

Still, honor your testy inner student. Throw your judge's graduation gown aside and toss your cap in the air. There's no need to grade your current status. Invoke your inner chancellor, committed to lifelong learning. You're not a cringeworthy failure; you're doing fringe-worthy graduate work. Whatever your present pomp or circumstance, it's here to teach you something important.

Earth School

Could fear this classroom session
Yet the part inside that's wise
Is convinced that every lesson
Is Divinity in disguise

I see the key is in nurturing me
And to give just what I need
Recharging inner battery
Inviting Spirit to take the lead

Now centered in the Presence
Endless energy coursing through
No questioning the questioning
When I acknowledge the God in you

Channeled Poetry, Winter 2006

BACK TO BASICS

Reuniting with my inner child was one of many unplanned gifts I received when I began studying early childhood education. I continue to marvel at the endless magical ways our playful innocence manages to reconnect us with our spirit, our awareness, our authenticity—our True Self.

Perhaps you, too, have deprived yourself of your distinct creativity. For some, this may have inadvertently started when you noticed your unique inspirations and aspirations were being judged or graded by others. At the time, you likely hadn't garnered enough awareness to understand that every experience is merely a learning opportunity designed to help discern future actions. Instead, you may have misinterpreted others' assessments, turning those experiences into excuses to disregard your natural inclinations. You may have felt coerced to conform or compete.

No wonder many of us unconsciously decided we had no choice but to join the self-judgment team. Perhaps we were led to believe we didn't have the wherewithal to be the leaders of our own lives. Being led by someone or something out of alignment with one's soul can feel heavier than lead.

Intruding upon the intrinsic ideals of innocence, it saddens me to think how we humans habitually expend our so-called adult years attempting to obey the idea we must take life more seriously. Working oh-so-hard, we watch color fade, helplessly witnessing as black-and-white thinking takes over. Devoid of gray areas in our minds, we obsess instead about the gray areas popping up on our heads.

I wonder how our collective classroom surroundings might evolve if we encouraged spontaneous, authentic creation to be itself once again. Imagine immersing yourself in direct experience, allowing yourself to become messy physically, mentally, and emotionally.

Playful and nonproductive, picture yourself being thoroughly amused by your ridiculous, no-talent shortcomings while your ideal audience, your classmates, cheer you on. You know, the folks who aren't grading you, because they, too, know the power of the sacred release of divine energy.

Learn the art of self-forgiveness, so every life lesson becomes child's play.

Stay connected to Me. Be My Hands, Feet, and Voice. Imagine Me working through you, so you practice teaching that to others.

— *G.O.D. Journals, June 2013*

STRAIGHT-A STRATEGY

Terms such as *report card* or *Straight-A's* might evoke a sense of foreboding within you, especially if you are one who relentlessly grades yourself for not being where you think you ought to be, or if you carry a false sense of pride, secure in the knowledge Ms. Information knows more than everyone else.

No one amongst us needs to *earn* recognition, so there's no use in endlessly degrading or grading ourselves. Being an advocate for authenticity, I'll freely admit I'm allowing the part of me who prefers alliteration to be an activist for the achievement of alleviating any abiding sense of academic guilt. Letting go of judgments provides space for innate wisdom to magically reappear.

Perpetually exchanging roles between student and teacher had me clamoring for a universal cheat sheet, since I frequently forget that which I'm sure I won't. Yet I can always ask for a new perspective in areas ripe for expansion, allowing altitude to adjust my attitude.

Let today be a day to start reclaiming an abundance of A's, in whole new ways.

Heartiest of congratulations! You, my friend, as a recognized ongoing honor student, are about to acquire six more straight A's.

And now, for life's testier moments, I share with you my personal study guide.

When ego is tempted to collapse into "cram it all," here's how to cram in just a little bit more willingness to gain a new perspective:

1. *Awareness.* Always the first step back into a higher state of mind. Gift yourself the awareness of this very moment, never to behold again. Observe current thoughts, emotions, experiences. You cannot embrace, release, change, or transform anything of which you are unaware.

2. *Authenticity.* There's no need to argue with fleeting reality. But it's helpful to know, in advance, how, where, when, and with whom you can safely share. Gift yourself the freedom of appropriate full expression that is harmless to yourself and others. Invite your body, your voice, your favored form of creativity to be momentary informants. *Pro tip*: Journal, shred, and repeat. Or write with your finger on the palm of your hand. No one needs to be the wiser, they'll just think you have a nervous tic. Who cares? Besides, feeling what you feel doesn't mean you have to—or get to—act on it.

3. *Acceptance.* Acceptance entails being present with all your current experience; physically, mentally, emotionally, spiritually. Put any thoughts of shame, game, blame, or acclaim on hiatus and embrace the temporary present. Honor the body's wisdom. Note momentary emotions. Embrace

neutrality. What message, metaphoric or mayhemic, is being conveyed?

4. *Alignment.* Your thoughts, emotions, and behaviors are just that: yours. If your default approach has been self-reproach, be aware of inconsistency within your heart. Feeling out of alignment is simply a call for attention. Congruence with who you aspire to be requires awareness, authenticity, and acceptance of that which is present. Vaguely or vigilantly, practice aligning your intentions from an ideal mindset.

5. *Ask.* All aspects of your A-game will become more enticing as you play with asking for Guidance. It's not your job to have all the answers. Your job is to stay aware and authentic, whether or not you are in current acceptance or alignment. Be willing to take a moment of inner inquiry. Ask yourself: *Who in me is currently providing my direction?* Lower mind tends to seek validation for its current position, whereas Higher Mind just might have another thought. Step it up by stepping aside. Let go of what you think you know. Ask for inspiration, then humbly consider receiving creative possibilities.

6. *Action.* Trust your Inner Knowing! Be willing to take direction from the Direction you receive. Remember, *doing nothing* is doing something—when it's done consciously. What if what you previously judged as *inaction* was actually that moment's divine right action? It needn't be complicated. Breathe. Listen.

Come back to awareness. What, if anything, has changed in your body, thoughts, emotions? What requires extra action, or extraction? Notice how the word *act* is lovingly embraced in both *action* and *practice*. No matter who or what we attract, or the ways in which we distract, any go-to tactic is meant to enact an act for traction. Regardless, make it a pact to remember this fact: The word *act* is most prevalent and most relevant.

Finding the treasures now ready to unearth themselves always starts with your awareness. In making the decision to replace reacting with playacting, inaction becomes impossible. Every little step simply leads to more information for consideration.

Come back to Me. Bring Me back into awareness. Ask for Guidance, then act. The results of the actions cannot be right or wrong; they are simply guideposts to deepen your learning. Action is the opportunity to practice trust. Awareness. Ask. Action.

— *G.O.D. Journals, October 2014*

PLAYING WITH AN A-MINUS MINDSET

Rudimentary isn't rude; it's elementary. Venturing into the unknown, you might be tempted to ignore the embarrassing bawl of the one refusing to move on. "But I don't know what I'm doing!" it cries. Not knowing how to handle it, you might kowtow to its sulking, retreating into all-too-well-known safety zones.

When the A-Minus Mind Circus comes to town, with its cast of not-quite-ready-for-whine-time players, prepare for an explosion or two. These a-munitions need to release some energy! Crankily cramming their way in and out of the clown car, they're argumentative, annoyed, avoidant, angry, anxious, agonized, awkward, aggressive, apathetic, and arrogant assholes. Abandonment issues abound; angst is likely in the center ring. When fools show up, chaos reigns, doing what they are wont to do.

On the plus side, perhaps exaggerated antics are designed to distract and to get our attention.

> Let go of the idea that whatever you are doing, experiencing, must be wrong. Your busy mind, the part that wants to hop out, is simply the voice of chaos. Whether in the midst of a circumstance or sitting in the silence listening for direction, your opportunity is to practice knowing that *I AM* with you always. Stay with this Voice of serenity. Trust. Relax. Notice. Practice. Delight in the life you have created.
> — *G.O.D. Journals, March 2019*

WHO YA GONNA B?

"Life isn't fair!" screams the part of us who knows it doesn't know. It doesn't know what's going on or what it's doing. Anger and fear arise every time it is reminded how very little control—like, zero—it has over life circumstances.

Yet life provides a great equalizer after all, my dear fellow beings. *B* is for *being*. Every one of us has been given complete jurisdiction over who we choose to B in every situation.

Fitting right in with your Straight-A practice, once you become cognizant of who you're B-ing, you'll notice Awareness has conveniently kicked in. Are you willing to B Authentic, then Accept what is so? Is your current way of B-ing in Alignment with who you desire to B? If not, are you now willing to Ask for assistance, and Act upon the directions you receive? Boundless within your mind, you can't possibly B in a bind. Whoever you

B in the present will extend into the future, until awareness directs otherwise.

Who you bring to each life circumstance affects the results. Empowering and enlightening, celebrate the fact that you get to decide who you get to B while life's happenings just get to keep on happening.

The part of you who still believes it is separate from others is but an illusion. However, it is no longer completely in charge, being out of alignment with your awareness. Mirages appear when you give them power.

— *G.O.D. Journals, June 2013*

C WHAT I DID THERE?

Who you B will surely influence what you C.

You'll C change when you decide to B change.

Put C first, if you like, so reaction can magically become creation.

Enjoy B-ing reactive. Get all stirred up, until you're C-ing the creative.

Creativity is fundamental.

If it weren't for creation, none of our perceptions would exist.

Reactivity is judgmental.

If it weren't for reaction, none of our deceptions could persist.

Learn to have fun with da-mental part of your mind. Invite new ways to C situations that seem to challenge you while you increasingly C who you were created to B. If all this seems frighteningly silly, gift yourself a moment. C and honor any part of you who might B scared. Can you now C that part of you as sacred?

There is a part of you who doesn't want to hear Me. It is accustomed to controlling, fighting for survival. Stop beating yourself up. Conscious listening is a new behavior, a new desire. Creative practices will strengthen the listening muscle, if that is your desired outcome. I become more audible when there isn't as much in your way.

— *G.O.D. Journals, August 2014*

JOIN THE SECRET SERVICE

Cerebral calisthenics strengthen mental muscles; so, how about a little extra-credit fun? Let's practice integrating our fun-da-mental ABCs, with an added bonus:

You get to focus on anyone *except* yourself.

Shh. Don't tell anybody, but isn't there someone inside you who truly loves judging others? From the privacy of your own mind, you have thoughts and opinions about just about everybody, don't you? Great! That's who you get to B for this exercise.

Bring to mind a Persy who draws out a distinct dynamic within you. An *energy evoker*, so to speak. Admiration or admonishment, unimportant. Present or previous, irrelevant. Fantasy or factual, inciter or inspirator, public figure or personal foe, no matter. Trust whoever comes up.

Got 'em? Good! Next, bring forward the part of your mind that feels triggered or touched by them. But please, for God's sake (and your own), refrain from disclosing to your quasi-qualifier that they are your momentary specimen.

Remember, mum's the word, especially if you've chosen your mum.

Depending on your story about them, you might suddenly notice yourself B-ing somewhere between provoked and stoked. Allow how you typically C them to support you in your present awareness.

Now let the fun begin! Pay attention to who *they* are B-ing while staying cognizant of the lens through which *you* are C-ing. Stay incognito! As we practice walking through our Straight-A Strategy, your job is to silently observe *them* through *your* playful eyes of curiosity and neutrality.

1. *Awareness.* Become aware of your already-awareness about their ways of B-ing—who you already think they are.

    What characteristics does your Persy embody? What about them irritates or attracts you? In whatever roles you typically C them, invite all nouns and adjectives to come forward. No need to redact, censor, or otherwise fib to yourself. Inviting all your private assessments to B a pathway into heightened perception; welcome in all those judgments, thoughts, and emotions. Fully allow yourself to become consciously aware of who you generally C them as B-ing.

    Next, consider how their B-ingness might change if you could C and observe them—under totally different circumstances that, up until now, were utterly unfamiliar to you. What sumptuous presumptions might you have been holding about them? Sans the role they play in *your* world, *who else* might they B, in a situation you may never actually C? Enjoy bringing a plethora of scenarios to mind. Go ahead, choose the ones that entertain you the most.

For example, if they are a co-worker, or a public figure, someone with whom you don't have a personal relationship, who might they B, how might they act when alone or with immediate family? Can you picture C-ing them sad, exhausted, nervous, vulnerable, sick? How about in everyday situations, getting ready for bed, brushing their teeth, interacting with pets? Try to C them in a situation when they are elated, having just received a surprise, or accomplishing a long-held personal goal. Who would they B during a therapy session? At a job interview? Imagine them being romantic, or in the midst of an emotional argument. How do they act when they feel insecure, mad, defiant? When they meet someone new, how do others initially perceive them? Why is that? What is it about their B-ing that others C immediately?

I know: You don't know. So, have fun. Guess. Make it up. C what you come up with.

2. *Authenticity.* Authentically examine your already-awareness about their authenticity.

From your observation tower, (remember, you get to make this up however you choose!) where, when, with whom, and under what circumstances is Persy most likely to be authentic, and a little vulnerable? What feelings come up in *you* when you notice *them* B-ing real?

Granted, if you've only experienced them when their neon sign of inauthenticity was flashing, C-ing them as real and vulnerable might seem impossible. Instead, you might experience a charge of superiority within, a surge of power. Go ahead, notice yourself delighting in watching them sour the limelight with their spurious stories while their barbarous body language gives them away. What do those compulsive talkers and constant interrupters need to steal from others? What secrets about themselves are they working so hard to hide?

3. *Acceptance.* Accept your already-awareness about their acceptance level.

Perhaps you've noticed how Persy's way of B-ing changes when they're fighting against what is so. Watching someone else refuse to accept present circumstances is an opportunity to cultivate empathy. We've all been in the state of inner battle when we've lacked acceptance of what we'd rather not C, and, as a result, stopped B-ing who we'd intended to B.

4. *Alignment.* Align your already-awareness about their level alignment.

Imagine for a moment your Persy B-ing in alignment with their Highest Self, whom they ideally aspire to B. While C-ing from your elevated vantage point, in what ways could Persy elevate their way of B-ing even further? What's missing, incongruent, gets in the way, or is otherwise out of alignment with their intention? What do you C about Persy's way of B-ing that Persy just doesn't yet C?

5. *Ask.* Ask your already-awareness about Persy's readiness to ask for Guidance.

Pun intended, what can you C concerning Persy's level of askance? Most of us doubt trusting others and, therefore, procrastinate in admitting a need for assistance. What ways of B-ing does Persy use to cover their insecurity? What secret stories would you guess their inner critic habitually tells themself? Can you identify with any of them? If you were Persy, what would *you* need from your fellow B-ings? Invoking your own Inner Guidance, ask for inspiration. From this higher perspective, what do you C as being helpful for your Persy? More love, compassion, support? A hot meal? A good therapist?

6. *Action.* Take action toward realizing your already-awareness about possible next actions.

What tiny next action does your intuition C might B supportive for your chosen persona? After all, you've just spent all this time with them. If you were to tune in to some Guidance for them, what would it B? Are you willing to envision them receiving exactly what you C they need? Might it B there are similar actions or practices that could benefit you?

Spend a few more moments with your Persy-in-Mind. Gently picture them at various ages, from early childhood to an elder. Continue envisioning them in a variety of human experiences while considering elevating your story about this Being's endless ways of B-ing. From rocket scientist to space cadet, it's only *your* mind that Cs who *they* might B. What thoughts would you like them to have about you?

We've all taken other Persy's personas personally, so consider what it is about this particular Persy that had you choose them at this time. What insights do you C, and in what ways has your perception of them, and of yourself, shifted since we started this adventure?

Could it B that Persy's way of B-ing reflects something about how you C yourself? Now that it's B-ing brought to your authentic attention, maybe you'd like to B more like Persy, or less. We build self-awareness by B-ing willing to C that our authentic assessments of others' ways of B-ing can B of great service in helping us to C the hidden sides of ourselves.

Damn those mirrors. They often show up in the most inconvenient places. And people.

Playfully—and privately—impersonating others under various human conditions can help expand our inner awareness while depersonalizing anyone's particular ways of B-ing. C-ing what calls us forward and what holds us back just might B a creative contribution to C every B-ing with a little more compassion.

Finally, acknowledge your Persy of choice for unknowingly joining with you and all the insight they provided. Invoke loving thoughts of gratitude. Maintain awareness as it flows through you, then extends outward, blessing all you bring to mind.

Congratulations! You are officially part of the secret service. What you give to one, you give to all, starting with yourself. As you practice increasing your awareness, authenticity, and acceptance, you will become more aligned with your own inner callings—humbly asking for, and acting upon, your loving Guidance. Start with awareness, then let the rest flow.

Yes, go within, Child. You are being led on a journey you literally cannot imagine. Why not take the road less traveled, following Inner Guidance? The good news is, your Navigator is always with you. Well-worn worldly paths literally lead nowhere; you can only escape the world of irritation and upset from the inside out. It is your refusal to let Me Guide that exhausts you. That part of you who doesn't want to is just scared, afraid I might be right.

— *G.O.D. Journals, July 2014*

F IT!

F is far too F-in' fun to forfeit. Furthermore, who doesn't love dropping a fairly fitting F-bomb, just for F-in' effect?

Seems we all have a faulty default *F-it* type. In between fighting and fleeing, some of us foray into fawners, or freezers. That's cool.

Oh, wait. Maybe you made up a story about which F-in' F-word I was referring to.

Fear is feasibly the most frequent, being the flunky that facilitates the false self. Fear's fondness to C almost everything as B-ing F'd-up further forestalls facing its own frightful fact-checking; preferring to forgo facing the fact that its false perceptions aren't actually actual, factual, or frightening after all.

Ever notice how fluctuating feelings frequently facilitate fretfulness, feistiness, and fussiness? Frantically fighting for relevance, the fractionated mind starts freaking out. Following a fast track to fury, its fanatic ferocity fuels the fancy to force additional fakeries. Folding under the fright of facing forgotten, yet familiar, fugitives, fields of fictitious figures emerge, furnishing the favor to fixate on future fantasy instead.

This habit of frenzied yet frequently fruitless feeding on such frivolous fare just might be forfeiting my serenity. Focus fading, fast.

All facetiousness aside, when I forget or forgo my faith, life can, indeed, seem futile and fallible. Fortunately, feigning flippancy while flipping out just might be furnishing a fix. I can always fake a mindset of flexibility amidst fluctuation while waiting for fate to play out.

I remind myself forgetfulness isn't failure. Fame and fortune are fickle foes. Besides, all forms inform, here to foster my awareness that I've merely foregone that which needs to B my utmost fundamental focus: forgiveness.

You need not even ask for forgiveness, for it is already done. You do, however, need to accept what is always, already yours, by giving it to others. Accept the gifts *I AM* giving you, Child. Your resistance to receiving serves no one.

— *G.O.D. Journals, May 2019*

Frankly, compared to our most familiar F-it mindsets, forgiveness may not be foremost in our default foray. In fact, perhaps our consistent resistance to forgiveness is due to the fact that ultimately, all true forgiveness requires self-forgiveness.

Forgiving is literally that: *for-giving*. What we give to one, we give to all, including ourselves. For what we give must come from within.

Awareness of the thoughts, emotions, and actions we've been fertilizing is part of the growth process. Ask yourself, *Sow, what now? Do I want what I've been reaping?*

Now is always the season for farming a forever-friendship with that most favored part of yourself — one who supports you in growing your own inner freedom. This requires cultivating the giving fields of guilt-free living while planting the seeds of forgiveness everywhere. Facilitate future foresight. Treasure the findings found only in frequent self-forgiveness.

You just might ferret out an unfathomable fact: There was never anything to forgive.

Forgive yourself. Be kind to yourself first—so you can hear My Voice. It is in the gentleness to yourself that you become gentle with others. Practice, Dear Child. It is your own willingness that will set you free.

— G.O.D. Journals, September 2018

IT'S OKAY TO P

Every Persy has the propensity to P, possibly more persistently than preferred.

A not-for-profit prophet Persy is present, proclaiming:

1. Persistent prissiness or pissiness perpetuates procrastination.
2. Presence, possibility, and perseverance propagate playful participation.

Peek-a-Boo, it's playtime! Who in you pretends to hide? Who has a preference to seek?

We progressive perfectionists have predisposed places where provocations and progress intersect. Pondering is profitable. If we've been pleasing plastic, pliable personalities, or possibly parents, perhaps it's time to pause a pattern in progress in order to progress. Portraying predispositions that no longer align with our preferred philosophy is prone to producing parables of pride, peril, privilege, and panic.

Pretense is nonsense. It makes no sense to plan to perform, merely making oneself tense in advance. Attempts to tend to something before its time is pre-tending, probably predesigned to preclude tending to the present, leading to more procrastination.

Once we C our programmed perceptions as planted in past performance, pointless ways of B-ing need no longer B projected into the future.

See how much we P? Speaking of such . . . okay, I'm back.

Profound possibility is profoundly possible! Prayerful pep talks with your preferred Pilot is powerful practice, so please, play with your profundity.

Fighting for Past Future Tense

Fighting for past future tense
A stress not well disguised
Project, obsess, on thems *and* theys
While asking endless whys

Opposing mental combat zone
Duality dubbed as right
A collusion revolution
Duel darkness dressed as light

Addicted to the war within
Cause avoids the realize
Judgment, fear, guilt, and shame
All mask authentic I's

Exhaustion did annihilate
A besieged battle cry
Balance begs for willingness
To release what now must die

Integrity restored equanimity
Awakened truth pro-found in lies
Surrender recharged unanimity
Amongst ashes, apex rise

Channeled Poetry, July 2008

THROUGH WHICH I ARE YOU C-ING?

Whether dueling with duality or rebelling against reality, keeping an eye on inner icons requires your involvement. Identifying the I's who are so full of resistance can seem intimidating. Yet the voice of persistence is consistent in insistence: "Now's your only time for peaceful co-existence."

Perhaps ignorantly, I imagine we all share something in common called *common sense*. But who amongst us commoners are uncommon enough to decide what is actually sensible? Accuracy argues that what one declares as *true* is often only their momentary perception; prone to being based in prior moments, perhaps littered by Ms. Representation, Ms. Interpretation, or Ms. Understanding.

In this age of incessant information, we won't always agree on *truth*. But someone has to be right, right? And, that someone, of course, is invariably I. Sayeth everyone.

Come on. Surely, you've heard yourself declare: *When* x *happens, then I'll feel better!* Wait a second—why must you wait for *x* in order to feel better? Who makes those decisions? Similarly, hearing yourself utter: *I wish I had/hadn't x-ed* is implication for inquisition. Which *I* inside is wishing, and which *I* does it wish to chide? Which *I* is responding, and which *I* wants to hide?

Prepare yourself. The next couple of paragraphs are intense. Intentionally so.

Incidental inequalities equal incredible insight. Who inside is telling you *what* to do, and who is telling *on* you? It could be that self-aggrandizing inner geezer, the arrogant one who likes to be recognized as the In-telli-Gent. Insufferable, really, and ironically, not in the least bit gentle.

Infiltrating incompletions invite irresponsibility, intoxication, incrimination, and indigestion. Infuriation, intimidation, indignation, and impudence intensify via impulsive ideology.

Interrogation, injustice, and injurious ineptness intrude. Incensed imaginings inflate. Incidents of iciness, isolation, and irritability increase—inevitably followed by an identity crisis.

Whew! Say that ten times fast. No, don't.

Instead, instill an investigative eye on the *I* who, in this individual instant, is implying—in fact, insisting—that *its* insightful interpretation is ideal. If intimidated by imposter syndrome, it might be idealizing its intertwinement with inglorious insignificance.

Awareness of current interpretations interrupts irrational stories, including the insanity I experience when interrupted, which boils down to a fear of forgetting that which I had deemed as incredibly important. Imagine issues indisputably initiating innovation, since retaining an incessantly incensed and irate ideology isn't the identity I indubitably desire.

Irksome incidents could be implemented as invitations to interrupt the intellect, invoking inspired insight. Although meant as innocuous, our inner involvement could be interpreted as iniquitous. So, let's illuminate our impediments. Instinctive, inspired insights from ingenuous, or, perhaps, ingenious, interactions are imminent.

In fact, Straight-A inferences are in sight, and ideally, insightful.

Our innermost saboteurs thrive on unawareness, inauthenticity, nonacceptance, misalignment, isolation, and inaction. Ego's insistent importance is insanely involved in its ignorance and indifference, invariably implying it must be its mirror that's backward. *If only you would see things my way*, it insists inside.

But you won't, damn you.

When defenses, disingenuousness, and discouragement dictate your way of being, it's an indicator you are about to become a casualty of your own commentary. The embedded ideas within our shared incarnation can leave us feeling like incarcerated inmates. Prisoners of the impossibly implausible. Watch your back, baby. And your mind.

The more illustrious *I's* I've imagined were inherent include:

- *Pissed-off-Princely-Princess*. Feels safest when trapped within a fairytale of fear. Lives in the Fantasyland of Tomorrowland while begrudgingly waiting for the Late Knight Movie, whose tarnished armament is a guaranteed no-show. So much for happy endings.

- *Artful Dodger*. A creative, nimble rebel, addicted to unfounded perfectionism. Thrives on excuses and procrastination. Walks around craft stores for hours, obsessively not-deciding on the perfect way to spend a single-use 40 percent off coupon for an item that won't get used. Strategy: *Thinking about doing things is the same as doing them.*

- *Captain Codependency*. Plays pirate-in-chief. Facilitates avoidance by vacillating between its *Aye-matey!*-people-pleasing-energy-pirating persona versus the never-say-nay naysayer. Reigns control from ye olde crow's nest, keeping a watchful eye out (the other is patched) for swabbie's next slip-up. Guaranteed to drive ye nuts while steering ye right into the storm. "This pirate walks into a bar with a steering wheel . . ." Oops, never mind, almost went overboard. If you're compelled to follow that treasure map, look it up.

- *Ima Loser*. Speaks nonstop as a demonstrator for the false self. Far too into their victim mode to bother playing with a little improv to improve their awareness, they are hell-bent on proving to everyone life is hell.

Misery might love company, but there isn't a blockhead in your mind or community that has the authority to block you from accessing your innate, inspired, impartial, intuitive self. Nothing but your own imagination has the power to overpower your empowerment.

Inquiring who is in charge is just a matter of investigation. Open an inner inquiry; demand to know: *Who's in charge here?* Go ahead—start an inner revolution. Intentionally inaugurate it as a predecessor for inner revelation. Get the inside scoop on the poop deck, or the poop on deck, as the case might be. All part of the captain's job, right?

Why not invent your own I-way to heaven? Whenever you are ready to see more clearly, instill a new brand of I-drops. Inseparable from the integrated, invulnerable *I* inside, it's your indivisibility that brings you visibility.

Ever wonder why the word *I* is always capitalized in the English language? My intuition eyes it this way: an invitation to integrate a new ideal—eye-deal! Capitalize on it. B willing to C anew by immersing yourself in inspiration. Intentionally invoke awareness that the Ideal Self is intrinsic and instantaneously available.

Your infinite connection to your innate Guidance is your inheritance. Inhabited within is that insistent invitation for inquiry, informed by instants of illumination. You are here to intuit and illustrate shared ideals from your inspired imagination. Invoke that innermost identity! Initiate those insights!

Take heart—so you can stop losing your mind.

Because every one of us is a unique and precious pronoun.

Notice the capitalization of the word I which is there for a reason. Listen, Child; practice and learn. Being your joy teaches you it can't ever be lost.

— G.O.D. Journals, July 2014

CHAPTER 5

i wish, i wish

Life circumstances and events are, in themselves, neutral—learning devices to help you remember you are always at choice. What do you wish to contribute? More fear, anger, resentment? Or more love, compassion, neutrality, oneness? After all, this is your life.

— *G.O.D. Journals, July 2018*

Ah, wishing. Wanting. Waiting. But for what? Are we collectively waiting for the dress rehearsal to end, so real life can finally begin? Maybe we've been whiling away our hours, forgetting to confer with the flowers, getting lost in disdain. But then life somehow shocks us, to awaken and unblock us, so we'll finally use our brain.

I hope you sang those last two sentences.

I'd like to think I've truly tired of wishing my life away, having squandered many moons while attempting to capture my heart in hopes of finally setting it free. Hmm. The very appearance of that random phrase strikes me as oddly oxymoronic. *Capture my heart in hopes of finally setting it free.* What the hell did I mean by that? And while I'm at it, what's up with the word *oxymoronic*?

Well, I hear my fairly prayer-minded brain reasoning, Oxymoron *sounds like a fool playing with a powerful cleanser. Your most valued treasures hide underneath what you're convinced is a sullied surface. Although corrosion and erosion haven't completely obliterated your heart, you must keep removing the rust if you truly want to truly shine.*

Wait. That sounds like work. No wonder wishing and wanting seem preferable.

Resentment builds when it seems time is being wasted. Ever been in a restaurant, wasting away, while your waist waits for the waiter? Seemed like forever, right? But it wasn't actually forever, simply because it isn't happening right now—unless, of course, you are sitting in a restaurant, reading this sentence, wasting away, wondering where the hell they went.

But lying in wait—as in lying down, or fibbing, while you wait—must have purpose too, right? *Crap.* Now honesty is insisting I call myself forward and tell you the truth. Only going for the pun potential, I didn't actually know the meaning of the idiom, *lying in wait* until a few moments ago. Here's the gist: *Lying in wait* refers to hiding, concealing oneself; watching. Waiting for a victim, for the purpose of unexpected attack.

Alrighty then.

Seemingly shrouded in shame, I've often misinterpreted scriptural teachings. A suggestion to "wait upon the Lord" immediately put me on the defensive, figuring I was about to be entrapped into doing something I didn't want to do. Little did I realize the suggestion may have been a gentle invitation to quietly stand by. Listen. Wait for inner direction.

Captivated by potential while paying penitence for the past, I've repeatedly played the waiting game, waiting for something or someone (else) to pull me out of perpetual perturbance.

For an exercise in humble awareness, reminisce on countless attempts to hold onto old thought patterns. Wishing for more keeps us entrapped in wishing for more. Wanting keeps us wanting and, ironically, often feeling unwanted. Waiting for change keeps us waiting for change.

And therein, perhaps, lies the profundity: lying in wait— for ourselves.

Not to attack, but to capture our hearts.

While the lower mind busily takes us nowhere, the wish, the want, for Higher Mind quietly waits. Now here. Ready to set us free.

Oxymoronic.

Your wish to help co-create heaven on earth is your declared Life Purpose. Do not let your ego's fear of being misunderstood, criticized, or disliked keep you from being in action, or as an excuse not to do what you came here to do. Your lower mind goes into protection mode, in the form of distraction, fear, lack of clarity. Practice listening more often. Procrastination only postpones; it does not alter your purpose. Observe the results of tuning in, trusting, and taking action. Today's the day.

— *G.O.D. Journals, July 2014*

PERFECTIONISM, PERFORMANCE, AND PRETENDING, OH MY

Critical thoughts are creeping up. Uh-oh. The hypervigilant child in me is immediately distracted. Likely stemming from that earlier stint on whiling away the hours, protective mind begins to chant. Straight from the 1939 movie version of *The Wizard of Oz*, all I hear is:

> *Lions and tigers and bears, oh my! Lions and tigers and bears, oh my!*

The most frightening creatures of all, those flying monkeys, are on alert. Despite my commitment to listen for the Voice of gentle guidance, primeval ponderings apparently still lurk nearby. Wandering into this terrifying territory known as the unknown, the demand to perfectly perform tasks I've never done commands commentary from my inner wicked witch.

> *I'll get you, my Pretty! Your thoughts are getting too close to the truth! Swoop down and capture them! Capture them!*

Self-protection is likely to show up in archetypal ways whenever new projects begin. Determined to keep me in a world where I no longer belong, inner Scarecrow doubts its brilliance while habitual self-talk insists it is scatterbrained. Inner Tin Man feels far from hallowed, finding hollow humility by hiding out in heartbreaking stories. Inner Cowardly Lion twists its tail while holding on, a little too tightly, to its longer tale of hurt, having been forced to put up its dukes and a brave front. And dear little inner Dorothy, well, she just wants to find her way back home, knowing somewhere, over the rainbow, there's an inner place where peace resides. She's been there.

I might be on a bear hunt, but I'm not afraid. Yeah, right. Sure.

Were you taught never to tell a lie? An important concept, to be sure. But by who's rules? What's in the F.I.N.E. (Fucked-up, Insecure, Neurotic, and Emotional) print? Oh, sure, yeah; I'm just fine, and don't you dare ask again! We both know any inkling of weakness is taboo!

If you learned to suppress, project, lie, and deny, then felt as if you must lie about and deny your suppressed feelings and projections—feeling crazy starts to make sense. You're in survival mode. Avoiding authenticity has become a way of life. No wonder you feel out of alignment. The repertoire of things to feel guilty about keeps growing, entailing a longer list of salacious behaviors, resulting in additional self-judgment.

You've always known what you've always known, yet you might have heard something like this, but intuitively knew they meant something like that:

THIS	THAT
Make us proud!	It's your responsibility to make this family look good, so no one will know how dysfunctional we are.
If you can't do it right, don't do it at all!	I don't know how to do it right either, and that makes me mad. Screaming at you is easier than facing my own inadequacies.
Don't cry; don't be needy, hurt, angry or sad; don't be too happy, loud, energetic, etc.; *or else!*	Stop triggering me! Since I can't allow myself to appropriately feel all my emotions, neither can you.

Time to redirect those monkeys flying around in our delightfully scattered brains! What the hell are they picking up, holding onto, then dropping at our feet? Poor old monkeys, they were only doing what the Wicked Witch demanded. They must have been terrifyingly terrified too.

Pretend, behave, perform, oh my. Ms. Behavior is tiring of attempting to tend, in advance, to the wants, needs, and whims of those who will never be satisfied. Ready to misbehave, she's here to speak her truth: The demand to behave is veiled vitriol, secret code for *be-have*. Be who I say, so you'll have all the love, approval, and attention you crave; that is, until you misbehave again. That requirement to perform, per-the-form of the controller's idea of *conform*, goes against one's natural form. Dealing with mold is no fun, so let's just break it.

There's no reason to perpetuate patterns of shame, blame, and control. Be kind to yourself; therefore others. Be kind to others, therefore yourself. Courageously share your truth, your vulnerability.

Let's heal the way for future generations, through our divine demonstration.

Feeling guilty does not serve you or the world as you currently see it. In fact, it is guilt that keeps you from your calling; a barrier you have set up to separate yourself from being with whoever and whatever experience is in front of you. Your interpretation views situations as something to just get through — to the next imagined illusion. Open the gift found in being with your challenge. Ask, and you will be shown the way. Be willing to release to My loving care the fearful blocks you have put in the way, so I can dissolve them.

— G.O.D. Journals, September 2012

STOP SETTING UP UPSETTING FORECASTS

Regardless of predictions, prophecies, and perpetual planning, the whim of fate has an uncanny ability to hoodwink. *Surprise!* The sun goes behind a cloud and winds kick up. The demand for certainty is certain to wind us up until inner turbulence becomes deafening. Echoing long-winded stories demanding attention, we must unwind from the bluster we've created.

Yet the vein of vanity runs deep. Perhaps the vane must blow in new directions for us to notice any overcasting signs. Overly attached to an egoic forecast, we may be unconsciously driven to control the uncontrollable. When awareness is outcast, broadcast from the inner lighthouse might seem temporarily unavailable.

But maybe unexpected storms are designed to startle us right out of preoccupations. When we've occupied ourselves, in advance of an actual event, even a bright forecast can quickly turn dark.

Once we get there, then this will happen, and we'll do that. But what if . . .? Then what? Should I leave? Give in? What if they're upset? Ugh, then it'll become a whole thing. What a hassle. Just thinking about it triggers me! Maybe I shouldn't even go. Hey, at least vacation is coming up soon. I can't wait, seems like forever! Weird, though, how it's always over so fast. Such a big expense. I always feel so guilty, spending that money. Especially after I get home, because then there's nothing to look forward to. Ugh. Now I'm depressed. Maybe I'll just cancel vacation too.

Sound familiar? What in us allows pointless conversations to be present in our minds when their only forecast is future misery? Just for fun (or not), cast that voice in a leading role for a moment. Notice its inability to find comfort or amusement in its bemusement about discomfort. See it for what it is: an attempt to usurp power by avoiding admitting its own powerlessness. Playfully applaud its proud diatribe.

Confusion stems from a lack of focus. Your ego will clutter up your mind with useless thoughts that have nothing to do with reconnection to Me, but where does that get you? Breathe in clarity. Notice what happens to your state of mind when you focus on clearing. Is not fogginess merely clouds, a mist? Be willing to experience That Which Is Beyond.

— *G.O.D. Journals, August 2014*

On those not-so-fair-weather-days (perhaps noticing resentment toward a fair-weather-friend) you might wish for more reliable ways to weather life's unpredictable storms. With a little more clarity and compassion, especially for your own tornadic reactions, you can increase your ability to calmly observe whatever's blowing by.

I just had an enlightening flash. The whether (or not) observation tower is broadcasting loud and clear: Strong polarities afflict our shared planet. Could current environmental, political, and social disparities be metaphoric reflections of a shared inner world? I don't mean to add to your pressure cooker, but if you suspected your unresolved mental or emotional storms might somehow be contributing to global extremes, would you accept an invitation to heighten your intention to discover which of your inner energy patterns were out of sync?

Maybe this is the perfect time to reacclimate ourselves to the Selves we came here to be. Rising above our inner clouds, a new perspective might become clear. Could it be that our personal incompletions, or collective his-stories and her-stories are demanding exposure? In ways we can no longer ignore, perhaps we are being inspired to recycle that which is outdated and to rebuild ourselves into more efficient, effective ways of being.

Unexpressed energy has to go somewhere, doesn't it?

Do you prefer upset? No? Well, why are you choosing it? The ego-mind can always find something to be upset about. Or it can be happy for a few moments when things seem to go its way. The constant back-and-forth in your mind is what exhausts you. When you begin to notice the upset, you are on the right track. You have risen above it, ever so slightly, thus gaining some elevation toward the willingness to choose a different mindset.

— *G.O.D. Journals, January 2019*

Most of us trust Mother Nature. Even when she's mad, we intuitively know Mom loves us, and naturally, we want to support her in creating and maintaining a healthy, loving atmosphere. Just wishing her kids would pay attention, though, apparently hasn't been enough. Time for some tough love. She's tired of our procrastination and is taking us to task. Gee thanks, Mom.

Maybe her energetic expressions are meant as a collective reminder for each of us to pay closer attention to the inner atmosphere, to where and what we are—or aren't—contributing. Being the Mother she is, she won't play favorites amongst her kids yet is growing increasingly weary of watching the fighting amongst us. The longer we ignore her, the louder she'll get.

No more fucking around. She means business.

The opportunity to experience profound inner and outer shifts are always at hand and in our hands.

What in your story is asking for completion, so it can finally be recycled into much-needed mulch? Nature will take its course, and harvest time offers great rewards, providing bountiful fruition. But we each need to do our part while accepting the fact that cultivating spaces for healthy growth takes time, commitment, and preparation.

In short, we all need practice in working with our shit while weathering unexpected storms.

If you were focused only on My will for you—on love, joy, peace, gentleness, generosity—there would be no fluctuation, no choice. There would be nothing to choose from, since Guidance would be all you knew. Why would you choose differently? As you see and experience what doesn't work for you, you will more consistently choose That Which Does.

—*G.O.D. Journals, January 2019*

WAITING FOR THE SHOWDOWN

Certainly, certainty is all but certain.

I'm *all but certain* this idiom actually makes no sense. Wouldn't *all but* indicate anything except? Certainly uncertain, I prefer to make my own sensible rules, thus often finding myself lost in the midst of quibbles with the English language.

All but certain (correct usage, 98 percent sure) most of us distractable free-spirit types aren't particularly thrilled with words that imply commitment, such as *structure, practice,* and *consistency.* Despite structure and practice having consistently proven themselves reliable reps for reaching revered results, a fear-filled, fault-finding rebel defiantly directs the drama with the dramatic declaration, "I'll do it when I damn well feel like doing it." Translation: *Not happening.*

Heavy sigh. What to do but take a deeper look?

I imagine we've all experienced avoiding being with discomfort. Expending precious energy, we tell ourselves, "I can't wait for *x*." But we're fibbing to ourselves. Not only *can* we wait for whatever we've been waiting for, we *must* wait for it.

Until—wait for it—we realize what we need has already arrived.

Fear of, or attachment to, a particular outcome can weaken our foundation, and structural integrity is a detail that cannot be ignored. We must practice withstanding pressure. Since staying wound around our wounds is guaranteed to keep us stuck on hold, why not use our time efficiently? Let's get to know the places where we wobble, so we can find balance.

Are you enjoying the Muzak? Or are you lying in wait, ready to pounce upon whatever's waiting for you at the other end of the line? Your story is important, but you needn't stick to it.

A willingness to stay aware of your way of being during stressful situations requires humility, strength, and discipline. Certainly, it's all but certain you'll need to experience intensity in body, mind, and emotions. In the past, this may have been the very moment when you gave in or gave up. Feeling far from committed, you may have considered committing yourself instead. From elation to emptiness, that desire to jump out of the skin can dominate far beyond a level of mere discomfort. I know, I've been there. Today.

But wait—we are now observers in the audience. We're watching those inner selves, showing up, showing off, preparing for a showdown. As actors, they're just doing what they do, living for being gazed upon with admiration and approval. Since our seats have cost us top dollar, we may as well relax and learn from whatever that inner show is here to show us.

I've always loved the William Shakespeare quote from *As You Like It*:

All the world's a stage;
And all the men and women merely players.
They have their exits and their entrances.

What if the roles we've habitually played, including those we've unwittingly allowed to play us, keep showing themselves to us for a purpose? In paying attention to each character, allowing them to have their say-so, we might notice parts of the persona habitually in competition. Each clamoring for their turn in the leading role, chaos ensues. *Heavens to Murgatroyd!*

Okay, Snagglepuss. Exit, stage left.

Begin to distinguish your varied controlling characters. Practice setting boundaries with those diva's derrieres. No need to stage any regret for your rotating roles. Audience, actor, director—learn to recognize and accept them as they appear. Yell *Curtains!* whenever necessary. Call upon the prompter to promptly decrypt any activating script.

Notice which characterizations are asking to grow. For example, should you have an inner cast member who is tiring of perpetually playing the asshole role, invoke further inquiry. Perhaps the thespian was holding an unconscious fear of ridicule, with no experience whatsoever in speaking from a place of authenticity. Recognizing ability, the one playing the role of director might slyly invoke a little triggering improv. There's value in random dress rehearsals, right? Even former assholes have potential for new leading roles.

Today's challenges hold great gifts, but perhaps to be opened in the future. So, be your own audience. Have fun in the process as you acknowledge, with gratitude, that this level of awareness takes, well, awareness. Authenticity. Acceptance.

Listen especially closely for the tiniest of characters, so they learn to trust you implicitly. They often speak in silent whisper, tugging at the tenderest place in your heart. Can you hear the epistle they emit? Enjoin, align with their courage as they admit, *I do not know who I am or what my role is.* Let compassion flow for, and from, the part of you who knows exactly what they mean.

Trust the present while loving the roles you've played in the past. Each has prepared you for how you are being asked to play today. Should a character show up who seems inappropriate for your current scenario, ask them to take a hiatus, or assign them an alternate role—one for which they are better suited.

Embrace the responsibility of being the director of your own play. Whatever your current drama, remember that asking for, and following, Higher Direction is an integral part of the role.

Be willing to call upon and consciously connect with Higher Mind. From a place of elevation, it becomes easier to observe. Not only are you removed from the interactions and reactions, but the roles in the play are revealed. Take instruction from your experience of peace. Discomfort might be your first reaction, but act from the gentle voice of comfort.

— G.O.D. Journals, October 2015

MOTHER, MAY I? TIME TO EVOLVE, PER-YOUR-MISSION

Whose permission do I need to experience the profound? Despite the desire to devote myself to playing with the profundity of the present, the fear I haven't yet earned it often holds me back.

I can't receive what I haven't yet accepted as already mine. Oddly, though, it seems I'm called to own it all: the shadow, the light, and everything in between. Could ancient beliefs about deserving actually be de-serving this evolving mission?

Alas, even expression requires awareness first. Next, authentic, vulnerable sharing. Extra credit points for courageously allowing these chronic thoughts of fear, resistance, and unworthiness to be heard and publicly acknowledged. Acceptance eventually appears. Maybe that's not exactly a reason to celebrate, but certainly I can find a little synchronistic sanctity in the recent rediscovery of the following 2014 journal entry.

It's never enough. I'm an approval whore. My productivity is being driven by wanting others' permission and praise. Challenged in trusting myself, my process. I can't avoid this calling much longer—nor do I want to—but boy, do I want tons of approval, permission, and guaranteed outcomes.

Misperceptions serve to consider new perceptions, increasing evolving awareness. The safety shield of inauthenticity is merely a caring cover, until a courageous decision for authenticity can be made. Nonacceptance is a protective precursor to acceptance. Malalignment waits for realignment to reappear. Surrender follows, perhaps unconsciously desiring clear permission to follow Direction.

What is your mission, your purpose in this existence? If you aren't sure, give yourself permission to ponder. Create a short declaration, in a form you will easily remember, ready to bring you back to center, supporting you in times of challenge. Here's mine:

Creative Servant

I am attuned to my Creator,
For I hear divine Inner Voice
I am inspired by such vision,
As I gratefully rejoice
That I am in co-creative service,
Because so deeply do I feel
The call, joy, and desire
To love, forgive, and heal.

Channeled Poetry, October 2005

Perhaps the gift of *re-mission* is divinely designed as a designated opportunity—an inspired invitation to honor and renew one's zest for the whole (and holiness) of their personal life journey, while Creator concurrently, creatively, communicates Its omniscient omnipresence.

It's been twenty years since *Creative Servant* presented itself through me. Although I remain devoted to my mission to co-create heaven on earth, that relentless call to reimagine triggers and trials as transcendent treasures hasn't exactly been easy. In retrospect, I can't help but wonder if the intention to be in co-creative service was a passive pledge to play with the profound, since meltdown madness has rarely found its own way back into metaphoric, miraculous metamorphosis. Solely relying on the manic misadventures of Ms. Adventure has yet to be enough.

When that enlivened Memorex moment magically re-presents itself, there's a flash of divinity. It's as if there's a soulful playback, here to gracefully brighten the moment—a re-turn toward a memory—mystical, melodic. The divine compass within is reattuning to the whispers of Guidance, reminding and encouraging: *Trust the mission. Follow your next Direction.*

The only permission you'll ever need is your own.

You are the one you have been waiting for.

You keep wanting, waiting, and wishing to be acknowledged from the outside. Forgive the small self. Ego operates from need, whereas Authentic Self knows there is no need. No need for fear, no need for acknowledgment. You are, as Love, already whole and complete. Practice living life knowing all as divine opportunity. Remember the Truth of Who You Are, so you will know it for others. Reframe permission as per-your-mission.

— *G.O.D. Journals, September 2015*

CHAPTER 6

whining and dining

Journaling is a journey, a trip to the unknown. An adventure to be discovered, a willingness to be shown. Listen to that part, let it all be heard. Surrender the embattled, release with solid word. Courage invokes curiosity; discover inner ear, practicing luminosity, sacred, ever-near. Justifiably fueled by fury, consumed with irrational belief, yet firm within this willingness, there's quiet promise of relief.

— *G.O.D. Journals, June 2014*

UNCORK THAT WHINE!

When I'm feeling lost, it's likely a sign I've been allowing the Chauffer of Shame, along with its copilot, Guilt, to drive the inner conversation. Interrupting the future or interpreting the past, the two of them have a way of taking me to places I don't want to go.

Still, the effort of finding a new driver, one who honors my desired journey while having empathy for where I've been, sounds arduous and annoyingly time consuming. Hearing myself whine about Shame and Guilt's work ethic rather than simply firing them raises my glass to the awareness that I'm actually keeping them gainfully, painfully employed.

Must be time to do what I do best: move from decanter to banter.

But first, a message from our sponsor, The Sobriety Sidebar:

Humor is intoxicating, so, cheers to all puns, rhymes, and metaphor! It's high time to embrace our long-awaited happy hour! Celebrating all of who we are, where we've been, and wherever we're going, let's toast to all within that needs only love and acceptance. No whine shall be left behind.

And now, let's begin our distilling process.

Start by getting still. Allow your premium, full-bodied whine to breathe. Invite any part inside that has tired of staying still to arise. Inner whine-o, come forth. It's officially whine o'clock! You may now uncork whatever's been aging you. To thine own whine be true.

A therapist once told me that whining was anger coming out of a very small hole. That made perfect sense to the younger me, who had long longed for unbridled permission to express all the fear, frustration, hurt, and confusion she believed she had to hide.

The very traditions we hated witnessing may have been dutifully carried on. As victims of those who were out of control, many of us resorted to intake, taking on others' controlling behaviors. We found ways to check out to keep ourselves in check. Despite a desire to cultivate the courage to open our mouths, we continued to shut down that which demanded expression.

Although our victim story may have become our primary perpetrator, we all have good reasons to whine. So, bottoms up! Let's put some fun in our dysfunction du jour and discover what's been fermenting in that dark cellar for ages.

Whatever you've been bottling up, allow it to bubble up. Practice being the strong voiceover for your hangover, or whatever's been hanging over you. Stretch that whine-skin.

Now, I'd be willing to wager there's probably some part of your psyche who absolutely abhors whining. So please, be sure to give yourself permission to whine about how much you hate whining. Then, gently remind your younger self that tantrums and meltdowns are a healthy part of growing up.

This whine class is not cracked. It's only designed to help us relax into acceptance.

I recently saw a meme (and just now noticed the word "meme" literally says, *me-me!*) that made my inner whine-o laugh:

EXHAUSTIPATED: TOO TIRED TO GIVE A SHIT.

I hear your sense of disconnect, your fears, your complete weariness. *I AM* with you. *I AM* also aware of your temptation to stay hidden there, but what is restful about pain and judgment?

— *G.O.D. Journals, February 2012*

DROWNING IN ELUSIVE FLOW

The call to be of service remains predominant. That is, once everyone stops pissing me off.

Living lies while pretending to live life is insufferable, yet suffering is something we humans know how to do, quite well. And, granted, it's easier to waste time doing what we know rather than spending endless hours failing at whatever keeps calling us forward.

Sans meaningful action, me-mean-meme-mind gets caught somewhere between obsession and concession. *No matter what action you take, it won't count, or won't be enough,* self-talk chides. But just noticing the juxtaposition inherent between most inner positions counts as action, right? Regardless, I hereby give myself full permission to at least count taking a step backward, away from that which isn't working, in my daily step count.

Depending on the moon—after all, I'm certainly not responsible for my moods, am I?—tropical depressions still spring up from time to time. Independent, unstable, random thoughts and emotions can tidal-wave me right into wipeout. Eventually, though, I wash back up on shore, culminating in a dramatic drowning scene. In full-on embarrassing beached-whale mode, ostensibly both terrorized by plankton and stuffed with krill, I finally surrender, forcing a grudging willingness to swish with salt water, twice a day as directed, for pain.

Despite mouthfuls of sand blocking my gullet, each voiceless tumble magically morphs me back into humble. As the internal low tide slowly recesses back, exposing my rockiest coastline, I notice a scattering of creepy, yet fascinating, sea creatures I fear will best remain in the depths of the unseen. Yet here they are, revealing what heretofore was hidden.

Maybe you, too, continually toggle between cosmic mindfulness and controlling militancy. The battle with physical, mental, and emotional heaviness rages on. Healthy habits suddenly become excessive and self-defeating. Sincere commitments come complete with logical excuses as to why we can't start until that elusive tomorrow.

We heal our past by landing in the present, right now, in the momentary discomfort of not-knowing. Since the endless thirst for need-to-know can never be quenched from an empty well, we can appreciate natural flow, trusting the trickles of whatever is springing to the surface.

Guidance always finds a way to garner our attention, even if we are not yet willing to reciprocate.

And that, my friend, is nothing to whine about.

That's right. Just breathe. Reconnect. Ground. The discipline of listening integrates your Knowing. When you forget, notice this: You don't forget for as long. Take Me with you. Operate today from knowing *I AM*.

— *G.O.D. Journals, February 2012*

STUFF AND NONSENSE

Your mind, like mine, is a storage container for treasured pieces o' shift. And maybe, just a bit o' shit.

Being the one who holds the rusted key, it's up to you to decide when to unearth whatever on earth you've been keeping locked up. If your treasure chest is hidden in a desert somewhere, perhaps in the middle of a *mine!* field — that is, the secrets it holds belong to you alone — just the idea of finding it, let alone taking on the monumental task of digging through it, likely elicits an urge to resist. Plus, the damn thing is heavy. However, if you have a sense that it no longer makes sense to hold onto nonsense — the stuff of inner guilt — perhaps the time has come to behold your innocence and unstuff your inner gilt.

I have a long history of difficulty in finding clothes that fit, as well as a well-ingrained story that I've never fit in. Funny how my mind gets odd satisfaction whenever I manage to force something into a place it's not meant to be. Figuratively bursting at the seams, clothes won't close, forcing eventual closet overfill. Maybe we should rename closet as *close it*. If whatever we've been trying to squeeze into, or shove shut, refuses to cooperate, it's a clue.

Something needs to be seen. May it tumble forth.

There is no need to judge the present experience. Be willing to learn from it, see how you might do it differently in the future. When your own stuff is being reflected, it is normal, and human, to collapse into fear.

— *G.O.D. Journals, March 2012*

Preferring not to bother with stuff that's bothering me, I'll predictably opt to be bothered by the word *stuff* instead. And oh, bother, brother, the stuff that comes to mind! Heaps of hoarding, littering life. Mounds of minutia muddling the mind. Unfinished business, unwanted heirlooms, unaired underpinnings. Well-seasoned breadcrumbs in a turkey's cavity. Stuffed Oreos.

There isn't much that couldn't qualify as stuff or, conceivably, be utilized as stuffing. Overstuffed couches (and pouches) provide excuses to collapse, reasons to lapse. Avoid the inevitable, until inevitably, one is required to move.

I tend to head down the excess expressway when feeling unfulfilled or overfilled. Plus-sizing things up, I have to admit it pisses me off that I already know damn well another helping won't help. Ever notice a correlation amongst wasteful thoughts, wasted behaviors, and the waistline?

Recently heard this in a recovery meeting: BINGE = Believing I'm Not Good Enough.

From doohickies to denials, we humans stuff the stuff we don't want to deal with, hoping against hope (hmm, another interesting choice, to hope against hope) that nobody (least of all ourselves) will notice. Yet ignoring becomes storing. Unprocessed stuff gets buried alive.

Eventually, though, too much to handle has to find a way to be handled. Overdoing the underdoing eventually provides . . . well, feedback—sometimes in the form of hating our love handles.

The weight of your fear is not a burden on them, it is heavy on you. What will change when you choose a lighter life? Imagine, envision, setting down your burdens and flying, bringing the light to darkened thoughts. Set down the fears so you can step into freedom. Weight is only in your mind, while Higher Mind is waiting on you.

— *G.O.D. Journals, June 2015*

OPENING THE CLOSE-IT

Let's talk turkey: Unstuffing stuffing behaviors begins when we cultivate gratitude, thanksgiving. We no longer need closet our authenticity. Well-seasoned, traditional recipes for stuffing our stuff no longer fulfills. It's time to leave the dressing rooms. Come out and play!

Opening our close-its starts by simply stopping. Stop stuffing your suffering by pretending to be someone you aren't. Stop punishing yourself. And for goodness' sake, please, stop stuffing yourself into places, personas, practices, pants, and pinafores that no longer fit.

You change the future by making conscious choices in the present. Your silliness, your stuff, your stories are part of your transformation. It's just easier to decide to be pro-fun while rediscovering the profound. Adventure starts by being willing to see, and sort through, whatever is in front of you while discarding what is no longer needed.

What treasures are peeking out of your close-it? What messages are they attempting to air? It only takes a sliver of silver light to enlighten life in a whole new way. Challenges are golden opportunities for alchemy. Your brilliance cannot be hidden. Uncover what you may not yet know:

Anything of true value will always be lovingly stored for you.

Your work needn't be so heavy, though it is what you must do.

— *G.O.D. Journals, September 2014*

ANYBODY ANTIBODY?

Opting to attempt for entertainment versus irritation, awareness is currently unveiling just how much energy the mind expends fighting the body. There's continuous competition between the various counterparts, all vying for control, each triggered by another's needy viewpoint. What can I say, except it's all a pain in my butt-butt-butt of constant distraction.

Finally focused! In the writing groove!

BODY. I'm hungry, tired and need to pee.
MIND. Really? Now? Why didn't you say so before we started?
BODY. Because I'm in charge! Watch this!
MIND. Holy crap! Gangway!
BODY. (Return from tactical facilities.) And ... scene. (Bows)

Body's whiny demands are pissing off the Mind. Mind, hating any distraction except its own, is irritated by Body's incessant insistence for attention. But where's that hate coming from? Ah, yes. There it is. Anger coming out of a very small hole. Seems there's a younger one inside, who, at the moment, has the power, but knows it will soon be slapped down for having the gall to interrupt the adults for being needy. Hmm. Gall. No wonder I've experienced painful gallstones in the past. Internet reassures me that, metaphysically speaking, gallstones are linked to frustration, bitterness, and emotional imbalance. Must be time to acknowledge the gall of bladder's blasphemy, justifying its absolute right to stay pissed. But do I really want to gain more pain? Besides, it could be eons before acidic stones of swallowed hurt morph into beautiful crystals.

Since I'm learning to listen, I'm trusting the body is finding gentler ways to be heard.

Your thoughts of not being able to connect are attached to fear. Oftentimes, the mind thinks it is too busy to tune in to the Still Small Voice. Willingness submerged, you felt lost. Underneath was judgment of yourself, others, and current circumstances. Yet there I was in the midst. You weren't lost; you were simply unaware of your priority.

— *G.O.D. Journals, February 2012*

Checking back in. Floor heater keeps legs and left arm comfortably toasty, but hands and right arm are miserably freezing. Irritation grows. Mind considers getting up, turning on central heat, which entails fighting with Body, who now prefers not to move.

Observing the ongoing wrestling match while hiking down the hallway to the thermostat.

Predictably, Body soon starts bitching it's now burning up. Watch Mind disgustedly mull over the physical, mental, emotional, and financial waste of energy while Body stands up, opens the damn window, and lets out all the physical, mental, emotional, and metaphorical hot air.

Irrational rationality or exaggerated emotionality, it's easy to forget we're all just spiritual beings encased (entrapped?) in a somewhat cracked shell, right here within the physical realm of basic needs. Cold shoulders prevailing, the biggest loser in this battle is focus. Heavy sigh.

It's true, I'm just your temporary Divine Vehicle. But that doesn't mean you should fill Me with fuel that isn't made for My engine; or let My fluid levels get so low. Please stop forcing Me to continuously run at high speeds that aren't safe, especially in questionable areas. Allow Me periods of rest.

Fill My interior with music, inspirational talks, fresh air. Keep Me clean, inside and out. Give Me trustworthy maps to follow, so I can take you wherever you want to go. I will tell you what I need, so please pay close attention to My check engine lights. In the interim, regular check-ins and check-ups are much appreciated. And yes, one day I will run the extent of My intended mileage, and we will respectively part ways. But as your current Partner on this divine trip, please keep Me consciously and lovingly maintained, and I will serve you well.

— *G.O.D. Journals, December 2014*

THE FORKED TONGUE SPEAKS

Maybe those tiny fancy forks are just metaphors to pay attention to the small stuff.

Every little fork in the road provides opportunity to taste possibility, despite a habit of biting back at unfamiliar offerings with self-righteous, private thoughts of *fork you!* Not a big fan of risk, I prefer personal guarantees. I want to be assured I'll like something before I try it. Writhing while writing out my irrationality, this is leaving a bad taste in my mouth. Better switch it up.

Pie-eyed (yum, pie-puns!) plausibility welcomes a delicious alternative: Piety. But this requires a slice of reality as well, since pie-in-the-sky ideals can easily be smothered by meltdown. Warm, sweet fruitiness, hidden underneath a cool-as-ice-cream demeanor, pious commands bake. Thou shalt savor thy crustiness and thy flakiness!

Hm. Demeanor. Noticing covert meanish thoughts designed to cover all that is triggering me, I need to stay cognizant of temptation, mostly in the flavor of demeaning myself.

Ravenous hunt continues. But for what? More stuff? More pie?

Nothing has ever lived up to its promise of perpetual happiness.

Even the fantasy of booking an extended stay at the gingerbread house no longer holds much interest for my food-obsessed inner kid, who still sometimes relishes the idea of using breadcrumbs to eat her way back home.

Even though trail mix makes way more sense.

How can we scratch an itch we can't even find? Seems nothing, nobody, ever satisfies. And yet, time after time, experience shows us: We're always being led in our next right direction.

Remember, Child, life is everlasting. There is no final outcome, as life must continue to evolve. It is your fantasies of outcome that upset you. Love might seem like fantasy—in situations that disturb you—yet only Love is real. Love is not the goal, but the reality. Learn this, and there will be no need for fantasy.

— *G.O.D. Journals, July 2018*

NAKED AND AFRAID IN THE GARDEN OF EATIN'

Speaking of treasures and stories and always being led in the right next direction, my daughter just sent me a timely meme: "Eating too much cake is the sin of gluttony. However, eating too much pie is okay because the sin of pi is always zero."

Creating allegorical versions of personal stories can be a lighthearted way to take a bite out of ways of thinking or being that are no longer in alignment with one's authenticity—or authority. The chimerical concoction that follows is not at all meant to be distasteful, nor disrespectful, of anyone's spiritual beliefs. It's just a perpetual stock of crock—or, if you prefer, a crock of stock—stewing around in my mind, searching for a creative way to sprinkle a new flavor on things that have likely been simmering for far too long.

Now's as good a time as any to acknowledge there's a persistent teen in me who is determined to make sense of the nonsensical. Constantly conspiracy-theorizing, she clearly needs to air some long-held grievances, having concluded long ago every so-called authority figure is hell-bent on mind control and fearmongering. Maybe this rant is a way to stop allowing hell to bend her mind. Yet rebellion and hormones keep her in a perpetually pissed mindset, particularly concerning any situation that remotely resembles unreasonable parental punishment.

Frankly, she's tired of that persistent feeling of guilt, which has her believing she's somehow to blame. For everything.

Although the concept of original sin has never quite resonated with me, apparently it is still an ultra-sensitive subject for my Inner Teen (who, just moments ago, asked to be called by her new nickname, IT.) Now, I can tell you, from experience, IT is generally a generous soul, embodying great respect, compassion, and curiosity toward others' viewpoints, but has little patience for those who refuse to return the favor. As you might recall, IT also believes in predestination; so, it's easy for her to logically conclude there must be sound reasons for any role created during a given lifetime.

Playful pondering also helps alleviate her anxiety, leaving her feeling somewhat comforted while entwined in vague discomfort regarding the purported details pertaining to the oft-told story of Adam and Eve in particular.

On a positive note, IT fully resonates with the sense of inclusion the story of Adam and Eve provides. If we can happily identify them as our shared great-times-infinity–grandparents, wouldn't that make us all potential relatives, with a natural propensity toward loving and caring for one another? But interestingly, wouldn't that also cast Adam and Eve in the roles of the patriarch and matriarch of the world's very first dysfunctional family?

Disturbing. Perturbing. Disconcerting.

Imagine: reams and realms of multi-generational guilt. Blame, shame, pain, burdened upon every shoulder. Those so-called original sins of our shared original Gramps and Grams—not to mention (except I just did) all that previously unspoken resentment for having been ousted from their lovely garden home—well, something's not right, right?

Yep, she muses. *Right from the get-go, we're all totally screwed.*

Hey, screwed, skewed, skeptical, or atypical, IT—who, apparently, by now, has been beyond and back umpteen times—is simply, innocently, attempting to make sense out of something she may never understand.

Really? she sarcastically intones. *How could, why would, Adam and Eve's pop, the ultimate loving parent, kick their creation, their beloved offspring, out of their heavenly home, for making an error in judgment? Banished, left alone to rot in God-knows-where? Abandoned, for all of eternity? That makes no sense whatsoever.*

That is, unless, of course, the whole thing was simply a big misunderstanding, a story passed down through the ages. Let the overthinking begin.

You have different frequencies and dimensions in your levels of awareness. You may not see yourself as physically there, yet concepts such as heaven or war zone make sense, due to the constant battles you fight within, as well as your experiences of omnipresent unconditional love. These very different appearances manifest from within collective consciousness; a series of individual choices that become (be/come to the) collective. Therefore, you need not see yourself as a victim of outer circumstance, because (be the cause) you cause your worldly experience by your chosen thoughts.

— *G.O.D. Journals, December 2014*

Admittedly, human experience never has made much sense, especially in the food and body departments. I'd be willing to bet dollars to doughnuts that every person interacting with this sentence has, just once, eaten or done a bodily thing some authority figure insisted was forbidden.

But hiding from Source tends to cause remorse.

No one must know what I did. Not me; not anyone! Hide the evidence!

Yet here we still are, apparently outlasting that fearful tale of outcasting.

Unable to abstain from familiar refrain, inner conflict renews, knowing that expending our limited time here on Earth arguing with the voices of gotta/can't, must/mustn't, should/shouldn't is rather pointless while guilt continues to screech in the background.

That burden of relentless shame is heavy, compounded by a constant fear of being caught in the act of being human. Can't help but wonder if the endless stuff we all carry—those long-held stories passed down through the ages—is simply insensible inheritance accepted. If so, couldn't we find a sensible way to disinherit it?

As I pondered the whole enchilada—while secretly wondering if I could also get away with a side of chips and guacamole—an inner dialog persisted, competing for my attention:

For Pete's sake (oh, wait — I guess it would be for God's sake, not Pete's), it was only a damn apple! Maybe Adam and Eve had a tiff that morning and feared being shamed by their creator. They probably didn't know how to sit with the feelings that were arising, which could surely be soothed by just a bite or two of something sweet and crunchy. Under certain circumstances, even the serpent of self-sabotage can sound oddly sensible.

"What's the big deal?" it hissed. "Apples are nutritious, and naturally low in calories!"

Right? According to most food plans, apples are an acceptable choice! Those great-times-infinity–grandparents of ours made a choice that made sense at the time. Totally understandable.

We sometimes get impatient with our Creator's plan and turn to forbidden fruit to soothe our fear of sitting quietly with the unknown. Maybe the whole thing is meant as a teaching moment: to ask for, and trust, Loving Guidance. To discern between the competing voices in our heads.

Speaking of such . . .

Oh, but wait a minute. Holy crap. I totally forgot. Adam and Eve were naked! Oh, wow, that changes everything. That's way more embarrassing. Fighting, eating, and na-ked—all at the same time? And in front of God? Now we're talking hell, for sure. No wonder they forgot who they were, where they were, so they freaked out, made a run for it. Who banished whom?

Pray tell, there's temptation in the midst. I'm falling prey to keep telling this ridiculous story. I feel my defense ratcheting upward. Admit it—anger feels so damn good sometimes.

What's up with that mean, shaming, parental pile of wrath, sneakily spying on them? Clearly dying to catch them in an act of disobedience, but why? That's not loving support, that's just damn creepy. God only knows where its own unresolved anger came from. Is it so pissed that it has to project punishment onto all of eternity? For an apple? Seriously?

But shit, there's nowhere to hide from that so-called god! Uh-oh. Now what?

Caught in the hellhole of my story, I have no clue how to get out. *Okay, okay. Just freaking surrender. . . .* Guilty as charged. Caught. Fully seen. Telltale chunks of apple between my teeth. I'm probably really in trouble now.

Better find a fig leaf to cover myself. But, come on now, seriously? Hiding behind a fig leaf? Who are we kidding here? Gaining more guilt by the second, now I'll need at least three extra-large leaves. Wait, hold on here a second. Fig leaves? That must mean there are figs here somewhere too. Ooh, I want a fig!

Uh-oh, I bet that sneaky-snaky-serpent, that voice in my head that tricks me into guilt, has finked to the food police. That damn ego-ophidian is a tattletale. Yeah, yeah, not only did I eat the forbidden apple, but a bunch of figs too. I can already hear my sponsor, Captain Food Fuzz, haughtily declaring, "No figs. They have too much sugar."

Everyone's always sizing me up, declaring my size is wrong. They watch, judge every move, every bite. Total invasion of privacy. No wonder I can't eat in front of anyone.

Now I'm pissed, and frankly, never did want to share my one measly, rotten worm-infested apple in the first place, the one that doomed me into hell forever. Especially not with someone I am being forced to procreate with.

Go away. I'm hungry. All these damn diet rules and stories I'm making up are mixing me up, making me nuts. Mmm . . . nuts . . . I want some mixed nuts.

Well, now. Did you see that? How the hell—for the love of God or the love of Pete—did my Inner Teen's goofy thoughts about Adam and Eve devolve into that whining-and-dining rant with a large side of guilt? Ingesting more guilt won't digest it, but experience indicates overstuffing myself on others' stuff will likely result in my own bellyaching.

Isn't it time we stop defending and abandoning ourselves? It's only quivering fear that keeps justifying the ego's overarching need to grow its arrow collection. Being what it is, it just wants to prove its perceived prowess by shooting an apple off of some poor unsuspecting head.

All that trouble, just so it can take a bow.

Trying to avoid your own Judgment Day serves no one. Hiding from the omnipresence of Presence gets old after a millennium or two. They say an apple a day keeps the doctor away. Maybe we've unconsciously embraced a collective rebellion against welcoming in our Inner Healer.

So, find your safe orchard, a place to air your stories. Delight in freely picking from all the fruit that remains for your enjoyment. Fortunately, life will show you exactly where you need to grow. But when we're only on the hunt for the sweet, we'll miss the savory.

The closer we get to the authentic core of our story, the farther the apple can fall from the tree—as needed, newly seeded. Whether sown or thrown, aren't we always in the magic of the unknown? And hey, even if you once believed you were banished from the garden, have you noticed how Love keeps finding a way to bring you beyond—and back?

The archetype of shame around the body is universal. Stop wasting your time fighting an illusion. Rise above your judgments and interpretations. Celebrate life in all its changing forms. See the wonder of creation. Demonstrate the effects of embracing the Spark, the Essence, the Is-ness of Who You Are; that is, the awareness of the Self beyond the body.

— *G.O.D. Journals, July 2012*

CARNIVAL RIDE

I'm incredibly thankful every time I reawaken from those very tiring dark nights of the soul. Deciding to play once again, I must park myself in a place of amusement, expectancy, and receptivity. One such incident happened over twenty years ago.

When we've been stuffing or starving ourselves right out of existence, it only takes a moment of accord to become aware of the discord of the competition within. Unsatisfied with life as it is, we may feel confused, lost, and empty, completely unwilling as of yet to take a new step.

Until . . . until. Until we tire of our story. That's when Creator creates a way.

Carnival Ride

Feeling fat and full of sin
Familiar fare evades within
Know-how knows I'll never win
But no harm in playing—let's begin!

Not-so-merry-go-round ride
Can't jump off cause visions fly
Smile defends the hidden cry
And fantasy's where I'll abide.

Feeling thin—it's such a high!
Though gentle witness knows the lie
Unfounded parts still sadly die
Divine diversion—shaky sigh

Not-so-merry-go-round ride
Longing for no place to hide
Denial still my trusted guide
Can't tell the truth to which I've lied

Now craving freedom from deceit
Yet illusion still—tastes so sweet
And contemplation—quite incomplete
Just start the race—despite defeat

Exhausted, bored, and full of shame
Nothing left, no one to blame
Ignoring odds, still play the game
Crazy wonder—results the same

Stop this merry-go-round ride
Whirlpool stuck in crazy tide
Yet hitting walls could be a guide
Through this mirror maze inside

Surrounded by divine embrace
For one another, hold the space
In gratitude for healing grace
Release the need for circle chase

Newfound freedom—enjoy the ride
Release the reins to soar and fly
Now present with a Loving Guide
Truth resonates—from deep inside.

Channeled Poetry, June 2004

those damn numbers

Defending against what you do not want through excessive planning, protecting, and controlling will only serve to distract and exhaust you, thereby increasing frustration, fear, and judgment. Instead, use that energy to remind yourself that life is much easier, and more fun, with a Guide you trust. After all, the scenery is always changing.

— *G.O.D. Journals, May 2017*

NEGATIVE NUMBERS

My relationship with numbers has always been argumentative. I don't understand them, and they sure as hell don't understand me. Mathematical definition of said quarrel: "An *argument* of a function is a value provided to obtain the function's result.

It is also called an *independent variable.*" Thanks, Google. Your definitive definition equals exactly zero sense to me.

My peculiar obsession with wordplay is perpendicular. Based on an angle that seems right to me, picking words apart and arguing with numbers somehow grants me function. Result: Void what I don't understand while giving value to an independent, variable, and opinionated ego guaranteed to be triggered when it hears the old adage *the numbers don't lie.*

Yes, they do.

Their relentless judgments and assessments keep me in argument, forcing me to waste energy trying to prove or disprove their validity. What gives some damn number the authority to calculate worth by the state of one's finances, followers, or fitness? Trackers, temperatures, timekeepers. Steps, sizes, statistics. The list goes on, ad infinitum. Can you even add to infinitum?

To infinity, and beyond. Numbers might be fair game if only they'd play a fair game. But they don't. Just in time for replay, I present another annoying old adage: *There's safety in numbers.*

No, there's not.

As soon as those damn numbers start talking and walking, hypervigilance kicks in. As one with a history of giving power away to bullies, those damn numbers are not only persistent in their pursuit, but they gang up and chase me down to catch and keep me in error. Their taunts grow louder, more convincing, more intimidating.

Then they have the nerve to give us grief about our ever-aging aging. Talk about another damn number. And another old adage to boot! *Age is just a number*, they say. Well, at least that old adage gets to be exactly what it is: Old = Add + Age. Maybe adding amusement plus a muse or two helps me zero out my numerical nemesis.

What energy might you free up if you stopped arguing for your limitations? What if you relied on My gentle Guidance instead, acting from that place of knowing inside? Trust all the right people, circumstances, opportunities, and breakthroughs are right in front of you, beside you, surrounding you, embracing you, as *I AM*. Breakthrough does not mean break-away. Embrace the present, and you embrace Me.

— *G.O.D. Journals, January 2012*

COUNTERACTION

How often do our number stories trend toward that which we would interpret as negative?

We can be positive about one thing: All numbers and stories are, by nature, in a constant state of change. They demand accountability, yet their reliability often proves to be unreliable — due to their instability. And that's a liability. Besides, lying to ourselves isn't likely in alignment with who we ultimately want to be.

There's no magic number or story that has the power to counteract a morose, melancholy, or miserly mindset. But being pennywise while noticing your momentary misgivings might offer a miraculous shift toward munificence. If your damn numbers and their chosen messengers have a knack for escalating upsetting power struggles, or rarely provide the loving feedback you crave, it might be a good time to stop super-sizing mesmerizing thoughts.

Take the scale, for example. In fact, please, take mine. The last time that miserable little metric moved in a direction I wanted was when I kicked it.

Giving that damn machine the power to weigh in on my worth, plus breaking my toe, equals kicking myself. Judging myself for its mirthless musings and my reactions to them is sure to weigh me down further. No matter what time of the month, extra expectations and ought-to's only add excess ought 'er retention and bloat.

As I kowtow to the demands of an annoying apparatus, its assessment of my ass means I'll either have to scale back on something I love or bow down to something I hate. All because it mirrored my interior fear of being inferior. Increasing the bulk of my resentments and guilt seems inherent in the weightiness of the secrets I carry.

Many of us have spent decades giving our mental peace away to a stupid piece of metal. Allowing inanimate objects to control our emotions and self-worth is exactly the kind of shit that weighs heavily upon, and against, us. Where on or in your body will that show up?

Still, moments of breakdown often offer moments of memorable breakthrough. Twenty years later, I can still feel pain and shame gripping at my heart, as I hid out in my car in the medical center parking lot. Despite the current health matter of concern, I couldn't quite summon enough courage to go upstairs, nor to just cancel the damn appointment.

Oddly, it wasn't the fear of the diagnosis that kept me entrapped, it was the fear of stepping on that damn scale. I was sure it had a personal vendetta against me. Refusing to downplay its numbers, it seemed determined, instead, to downplay the sincere efforts I had been making toward incorporating a healthier lifestyle while it delighted in calling me a liar.

But something shifted that afternoon. As I sat in my car, it suddenly dawned on me that this momentary awareness was inviting me to up my part in the game. I could continue to give myself grief, or I could embody gratitude for the body I had.

Fully aware of the internal heaviness I habitually carried, I decided to shift my shit and made a conscious vow: No matter what the outcome of that appointment, it was time to commit to complete love and acceptance for my body, honoring it for what it was: a temporary temple housing my spirit.

I happen to be a fan of the work of Louise Hay; and interestingly, the diagnosis and subsequent treatment I received that day had multiple metaphysical meanings: nursing old hurts, fear of letting go, holding on to old ideas, being pissed off. Metaphoric, right?

Life always has its way of pointing us where we need to grow while perhaps letting go of growths we'd rather not embody. Every circumstance leads us on our way, but it need not weigh us down. No circumstance, no object, no person gets to weigh in on our self-worth, unless we give it permission to do so.

So, please, stay aware of—and authentically acknowledge—any guilt or resentment you've been heaping on yourself. It might just be your next step toward healing as you step away from the heavy scales of self-judgment.

Surely, you'll soon feel lighter.

There is nothing to fear other than your own limiting thoughts and interpretations. Release their perceived power by embracing Mine. Stop wasting your energy trying to predict and control outcome. That only keeps you stuck in inaction. Let go of the results so you are free to know your next guided steps.

— *G.O.D. Journals, February 2015*

Weirdly, counting has never kept me accountable.

For decades, I bought into the Creed of Count: that counting calories, carbs, cash, and coins could somehow grant me the ability to counter and control all other controllers. Not so. Uncovering Count's lairs, where its liars lay, prompted me to promptly defund the trust fund.

I've decided to no longer worry about the time I think I wasted, counting down my precious moments in anticipation of some future moment soon to be replaced by yet another.

Castling within the walls of *too much* or *not enough* is no longer where I choose to stay.

Counts and Countesses, begone! You've become a royal pain in my ass.

Your inner kingdom is here to prepare you for your ongoing awakening, letting you know its desire for a changing of the guard. Desire. Must be time to de-sire those controlling inner entities that have been robbing you of your serenity.

Today, I'm choosing counterbalance—accountability and balanced choices. Any opinions about how something did/didn't, will/won't or should/shouldn't turn out shall now be counteracted by turning within. Which now shall officially count as conscious, sacred action.

There is a balance. The practice of listening and going within is the foundation. Your story of it doesn't count unless you follow certain rituals or somehow prove your experience is only that: your story.

— *G.O.D. Journals, September 2018*

NUMBERS ARE NUMBERS

Back in the day, we used to call a rolled joint of marijuana a *number*. Context is amusing me, as I notice the word *numb* conveniently embedded within the word *number*. Despite four decades of sobriety, the lifelong habit to *numb out* sometimes still seems preferable to confronting reprehensible, incomprehensible ideals, let alone heretofore unpracticed practices.

Especially when fearing the aftermath.

I must regularly remind myself not to be an alarmist. Raging at or racing against clocks, calendars, or life's circumstances wastes precious energy. My opinion about how fast or slowly things should be going is irrelevant. Whatever my current concern, I must get over it, go around it, or alas, rise above it in order to go through it.

Let's surrender our arguments with what is, so we can let go of our most prominent, problematic, and collective story problem: that irrational idea that we already know—or at least should know—the correct answer to any dilemma, in advance of the actual experience.

Wrong answer.

Your habitual tendency to judge yourself, others, or a situation as wrong is in direct opposition to connecting with Me. What if you were meant to share your experience of listening to your Still Small Voice with others?

— G.O.D. Journals, December 2011

DIVVY UP FRACTURED THINKING WITHIN
THE STORY PROBLEM

Fixations won't fix anything.

Yet here I am again. Watching divided mind trying to pre-fix the discomfiting, unfitting, discomfort within. Default mind mode begs to defend. There it goes, protecting itself. Digging deeper, it discovers dense, intense meaning in the word *division*. Brilliantly noting the prefix *di-* means "twice," it adds the word *vision*, equaling "double vision."

See the logic? Me neither.

But wait! My magical inner mathematician apparently needs to create an argument. *Double that again. Don't two negatives make a positive?* Duality, two parts, are inherent in both universality and individuality. If everyone would simply envision that, equating all of humanity as indivisible individuals, undivided in their intention for unconditional self-acceptance, life would not be so fractious. See, I pre-fixed it. *Whew!*

Trouble is, when I get lost in thought, I forget my part. Judgments of self and of everyone else prevail. Too many conclusions and not enough clues. Partial answers everywhere, all subject to growth and change, completely incomplete and rationally irrational. Back to questioning my sanity, I experience divisiveness and defensiveness within my ideal vision.

Is there any percentage of me who even vaguely understands what I'm trying to convey to you? I don't know the answer to my own problem story, so I'll just do what I know how to do: play with the word *percent*. Statistically speaking, there's high probability every problem probably contains an ability to convert this moment's story into an infinitesimal decimal.

Per-sent. For what purpose per-we-sent? Instead invoking the usual keep-the-story-problem-going answer of *I don't know,* check in with awareness. Aside from the fact that there's only a fine line between a denominator and a numerator, what's up?

Fractions, my friend, fractions. You know, those freakin' actions you avoid taking, so you don't have to walk through your fear. Yet whenever you take even a fraction of an action, you remember it's those fractional pieces that somehow wholly rearrange themselves into your next holy-shit clue.

Imagine if just ten more people cleared their minds every morning, then listened and followed their Direction. Of course, that's just a fraction of what I have planned. But even that minuscule amount, what difference might that make in those ten people's lives? What about the people they touch?

— *G.O.D. Journals, December 2011*

You are always the common denominator in your own life experience, so dominate it. Instead of de-nominating yourself, voting yourself out, or revoking your candidacy, be candid in your devotion to heartfelt issues. Discover your vote for divine connection was cast long ago, as maybe some decisions were never yours to make.

Pay attention to your mixed fractions. It's okay to be confused. Awareness of our shared wholeness requires practice. Utilize the method of substitution to replace any divisive beliefs with a deliberate decision for divine decisiveness. You can't do it wrong.

This I can promise: None of us wholly created ourselves.

By nature, you are forever part of That Which Created You. How, if at all, you choose to define that Creative energy is a very personal matter. Still, in every moment of sacred inception, there must be alignment, a blessed yes, to that which is being created, with the nature of its inspired creator infinitely embedded within.

Even if it's a tiny percentage, isn't there at least a fraction of an inner actuary, a reckoner in you, who reckons they have tired of trying to conquer and divide while fighting this complicated, ever-changing world of endless forms and numbers? Maybe that part of you is vaguely intrigued by the idea of letting go of the checkbook; figuring it might be time to check your accountability.

Although you are exceptional, you are no exception to the rule. No matter how you might define this entity known as *you*, you simply don't have the power to fraction, fragment, divide, or scatter the energy of your Creator, Who can, and will, continue to co-create through you.

If there's shit you are ready to shift, accept an invitation to start treating the Creator part of your mind with a little reverence. Ask It, your Source, for guidance while taking responsibility for the source of your upset. Then the forgiveness piece of your work can begin. No matter what your story, you needn't be a problem, Child.

Replace your judgment with curiosity. Judgment implies you already know what you think the outcome should be. How could you? Open your mind, Child. If your thoughts don't invoke feelings of peacefulness, joy, and freedom, know there is higher knowing. Be willing to consider asking for a different vision, as opposed to the division that haunts you.

— *G.O.D. Journals, January 2016*

EXPONENTIAL PUN POWER IN MATH METAPHORS

Disconcertion with any number might lie (yes, lie) within a personal refusal to acknowledge cause. Fibbing to ourselves is a common human trait. Who wants to admit their part in how that number they'd rather not see got to where it is? Who likes seeing the futility in rebelling against absolute numbers over which they have absolutely zero control?

Since our days are numbered, how many more shall we expend in being concerned about that which we cannot know? I don't know about yours, but my inner Ms. Calculator tends to miscalculate the importance of events that may, actuarily, never happen.

If you're entrapped in allowing current numbers, statistics, or other mathematical mental gymnastics to drive your emotional well-being, consider which unconscious exponential powers may have been in play. Who, or what, are they?

Next time you notice your mind or mouth taking off on one of its tangents, consider the possibility that biased basis is basically based in the past. Conclusions drawn today may no longer apply. Instead, let's co-create new ways to dig for buried treasure.

What if our story problems could be easily resolved, simply by taking an honest look at our typical orders of operation? Consider enjoying the process of finding those puzzling pieces o' shift. Experiment with putting together the pieces you have in creative new ways. Your variables, your choice. For example, here's a little game I just made up:

Let w = the variable, any who/whom or what of your choice, then put an inner inquiry into operation.

1. W comes first? (When? Where? Why? Under what circumstances?)

2. *W* do you put into parenthesis, put on hold, think of as optional? (Why?)
3. *W* brings up feelings of division? (Why? When? Where?)
4. *W* in you is requiring < or >? (Multiplication? Subtraction? Addition?)
5. *W* is vociferating for complete erasure? (Why? And, maybe, when?)

Regardless of infinite thoughts about finite numbers, embracing facts is always a viable option. Numbers are what they are, but only momentarily, basically rendering them meaningless. They may have been graced with the title of infinity, but their message is wholly neutral. Simply information. Feedback. A snapshot in time. An invitation: What's next?

You might find there are great returns to be gained on thought investment. Capitalizing on the idea that no number has the power to either elate or irritate, spend some time recalculating how much energy you are willing to continue to invest in your insecurities. Since you are a product of Creation, there is infinite security to be found in the precious treasure of you. All you will ever need in this moment is already yours, here in perpetuity.

Time won't stand still, so still the mind instead. Update your life's portfolio. Take stock of your beliefs. Shift things around. Get expert advice. Be accountable to your authenticity. Build new equations. Multiply your independence, values, and function, and delight in new solutions.

Maybe those damn numbers aren't quite so permanent, relevant, or important after all.

Tuning into the Inner Voice only seems difficult. When you are focused on the distractions, that is what you are choosing. When you focus on the Silence, It becomes more audible. Here in the Silence, you hear My Direction. The real question is: Will you choose to practice, even when you perceive it as difficult? That's right; take a deep breath, and breathe that in. Circumstances need not direct your choice; rather, let commitment drive your decision.

— G.O.D. Journals, June 2014

CHAPTER 8

shaping up

Become aware of the burdens you are carrying—so you will decide to release them to Me. Notice how the tension in your body dissipates when you let go of your thoughts and move into deep listening. Defense and worry are impossible when you truly surrender. Allow this moment's experience of relaxation, serenity, and peace in your body to become a catalyst, a reason, for more frequent practice.

— G.O.D. Journals, January 2019

ALIGN WITH BEING OUT OF LINE

What's your right angle?

In a form that's unique, each of us is here to reflect the light; to be the prism we are.

Did you ever intentionally make yourself dizzy as a kid, or perhaps play games that required you to walk backward or wear a blindfold? You may have had to trust someone to catch or steer you in a safe direction. Even if playmates or siblings didn't keep their part of the bargain, you still survived. Back then, letting go of control and having no idea where you were going and if or when you'd fall, let alone where you might land, was all part of the fun. In fact, it was probably the whole point of the game.

Yet somewhere along the line, most of us stopped playing with the unknown. Perhaps we were teased, shamed, or betrayed by those we thought we could trust. Instinctual survival skills kicked in, and we learned all kinds of creative ways to protect ourselves from the unexpected.

Despite my chronically round shape, I'm prone to triangulating, surely squarely rooted in my tendency toward codependency. While mired in the belief that others saw me as obtuse, I began to observe parallels that didn't quite line up. Although I may never understand cosine, today I can no longer cosign thoughts and behaviors that just don't align. Notwithstanding silly word play, learning to accept right-for-me angles continues to be a circular and exhausting process, although circumcenter to my foundation. The shape of my heart is up to me.

Frequent summoning by my childhood commanders-in-chief to "shape up or ship out" would kick me right into checking out. *Abandon shit!* No thoughts or feelings of my own allowed. But now, check this out: Today's right-angle-interpretation-for-me is to welcome in the tendency to check out, as being in perfect alignment, parallel to my purpose.

That is, as long as I stay willing to check in, first.

Let go of the judgment while staying aware you are making a conscious choice. Whether you choose to go forward with *checking out* is beside the point; rather, cultivate this opportunity for awareness. No matter what form you use to check out, isn't your real intention to check in, looking to realign with your Inspired Self?

Maybe foresight needn't always wait for hindsight. My inner rule-follower has been shaping up to become an epic, rebellious, rule-breaker. In fact, she's probably the one who's writing this book. She got tired of waiting her turn. For what, I'm still not sure.

The Check-Out Line

I was standing in the check-out line
Like I'd been taught to do
Obediently following directive
Of everyone named you

Feeling kind of fidgety
Seeking new in-line distraction
Hoping someone, something, somehow
Could buy perpetual soul satisfaction

Handing the cashier my money
While resenting she stole my time
I left that store, still hungry for more
And got in another line.

Channeled Poetry, Spring 2005

CARVING UP CIRCULAR THINKING

The bored fourteen-year-old in me was probably doodling, wasting time with her crazy collection of colored pens, when a quirky desire to try her hand at writing backward appeared. Entertained and elated that the ability came quite naturally, by the grace of the predestination Gods, later that same year, I landed a coveted space in a folk arts class. This served not only to support me in avoiding academics, but conveniently just happened to include a unit in linoleum carving and block printing. I guess it's my destiny to look at life and letters in a backassward way.

Sending you back to your youngest innermost knowing, did you ever feel as if you saw or felt things others didn't? Confused, maybe you wondered if you landed in this life by mistake, were placed with the wrong people, or were somehow on a weird mission to bring them a message.

Alas, if only we knew the right words would appear in the right moment, so the knowledge, gifts, talents, and longings of the heart we all possess could be shared. If only we could finally hear and honor each other, so the validation we are all seeking would finally, undeniably, be ours.

Ready or not, the unresolved past keeps showing up when it's ready to resolve. So, please forgive this spontaneous venture into additional transparent tale-chasing.

No matter what you are doing, when it's based in fear, your tasks seem more difficult. It's the ego's nature to project, blame, shame; to be a victim or superior, to tell stories over and over. Listen, my Child, Listen.

Listen deeper. You are here to practice listening at a deeper level. Not to the ego, but to Me.

— *G.O.D. Journals, March 2012*

Fast-forward four decades. The passing of the final parent of a generation is apparently an ideal opportunity to deal with those parenthetical matters.

Although we were all officially old enough to be deemed members of the dreaded Establishment, nothing could change the fact that I remained the youngest among those who—like it or not—had become the family elders. And yet, given the fact that I was the only one with decades of sobriety and therapy, plus training in spiritual psychology, surely no one else was more qualified than I to step into the role of Family Fixer.

I was certain others would want the freedom I had found. Besides, for the sake of multi-generational healing, it was high time I put on my big-girl panties and facilitate a long-overdue discussion. It was my job to bring the ongoing family dysfunction to the forefront while creating a safe space to speak the unspeakable. After all, the retelling of old hurts, resentments, and misunderstandings is a necessary step before letting them go.

Imagine the love fest we'd share after everyone had their turn to air their hurts, interpretations, and misunderstandings that had kept them stuck in addictions for years. We'd all have a good cry, finally feeling relatively safe with relatives—to whom we could now relate. Our expanded heart space would create room for the dawning of a new understanding. Family dysfunction is a no-fault dilemma, necessarily fully forgivable for one's own peace of mind. Dutifully honoring *our* elders, we'd be the kin, the kindred spirits, who finally did what those before us could not: Be real—and heal. We'd teach our kids it

146

was okay—and necessary—to be authentic, to have difficult conversations. We'd make the difference for generations to come, and we'd all live happily ever after. For eons. Yes indeedy, this "Mar-Eon" does see eternity.

Except. Not everybody sees things like I do.

When you are attached to your perception, you cannot know Truth. Your judgment of this situation becomes your distraction, your unwillingness to be shown. Know that there is Light to show you the way, but you must be willing to access it. You cannot simultaneously hold onto your dark thoughts without expecting a shadow. Open to re-mind, Dear One, and let My Light pour in. Be willing to listen, to look, to love. Notice that when you do, the peace you seek is already here.

— *G.O.D. Journals, October 2014*

In an instant, my idea of illumination turned to illusion. Nothing had changed. Not only was there no wise elder to back me up, but these newly appointed elders had no inclination whatsoever toward reconciliation. Still, I tried to give them the benefit of the doubt.

Unable or unwilling to face the damage they, too, had endured, maybe they allowed their unconscious projections to perpetuate in perpetuity. Their habit of teasing and torturing the youngest, burying the wisdom, the knowing—and the hurt—of *their* younger ones inside was something I could understand—and forgive.

Still, how did they have the nerve to continuously cite their version of religion while engaging in unkind and unscrupulous behavior? While busily criticizing my beliefs in karma, they focused on what we could never take with us. When one is being driven by the monetary and the material, it seems there is no time to honor the momentary or the memories. Clearly, we were at odds.

I was heartbroken and confused. My thoughts of devotion to one another had gone from deemed to doomed, and I collapsed into concession. Their love, approval, and understanding would never be mine. I would forever remain unseen, unheard, unimportant, overpowered, and undervalued. Encompassed by inner compass, I sadly watched my family fantasy fade into nothingness. Time to escape to my dark place, where tears could privately fall.

INCITE TO INSIGHT

The garage of my 1960s childhood had served as both playroom and storage space. To the best of my knowledge, it had never housed electricity, let alone a car. The only source of natural light was the doorway leading in. Literally and metaphorically, I stepped into the dark past.

The black tar paper–covered wall still held my secret, right where I had left it, in faded white chalk. Now barely decipherable, in what must have been a courageous flash of self-expression nearly a half-century earlier, the childish scrawl was still poignantly present, entrenched in the emotion behind it:

NOONE LOVES ME.

As my inner child magically reappeared in my mind, I watched her curiously peer up at her creation. While sadness

148

wrestled with savvy, she somehow knew something wasn't quite right. The passion was accurate, but "noone" left her feeling oddly unsettled about the newly learned rules concerning compound words. Not that anyone cared, not even Peter Noone.

But who knew, maybe something told me I was into something good.

From reverie to recognition, I realized this moment of retreat from current family drama was a grand act of self-care. It was as if a loving guide had taken over, perhaps that courageous younger one inside, leading the way. A journey back into our secret, sacred space, right into enlightenment.

With renewed strength and courage, I decided to stay on course and follow my heart. Finding my flashlight, I carefully made my way back to the darker recess of both garage and memories. Perhaps the love I feared had been lost forever was still full of life, right there waiting for me.

Intuitively, I reached into the side cupboard of the big cabinet. My faithful fantasy friends—Archie, Betty, Veronica, Reggie, and Jughead—were alive and well, still immersed in their comic book teenage romance and drama at Riverdale High. Sporting mod attire in bright colors, bell bottoms, and go-go boots, they were still wreaking havoc for Mr. Weatherbee and Mrs. Grundy, while sea monkeys and X-ray specs could easily be procured for under a buck.

Maybe the idea of *nothing ever changes* wasn't such a bad deal after all.

Vintage copies of *Mad* magazine brought a much-needed smile to my face. My eye for detail still attuned immediately to the amusing drawings in the margins. Next, I instinctively turned to my favorite section, *The Lighter Side Of . . .*, followed by checking to see which movie or television show was the victim of the satire-of-the month, such as, *Makeus Sickby M.D.*, a parody of the TV series *Marcus Welby, M.D.*; or *The Odd Father*, a parody of *The Godfather* movie, circa early 1970s. The literary works that influenced my sense of humor is becoming clear.

Memories of safe and sacred escapes during the innocence of the wonder years began to unblock themselves. No cigarettes, drugs, alcohol, or boys allowed.

Sensing there was more, I reached farther into the cupboard. Out rolled (well, not really, but the visual is more dramatic, versus saying "there I found") my old paint brayer, specifically purchased for that linoleum carving/block printing class. Beside it, a stack of my block creations.

One in particular gifted rare insight into the mind of my heretofore forgotten inner teen:

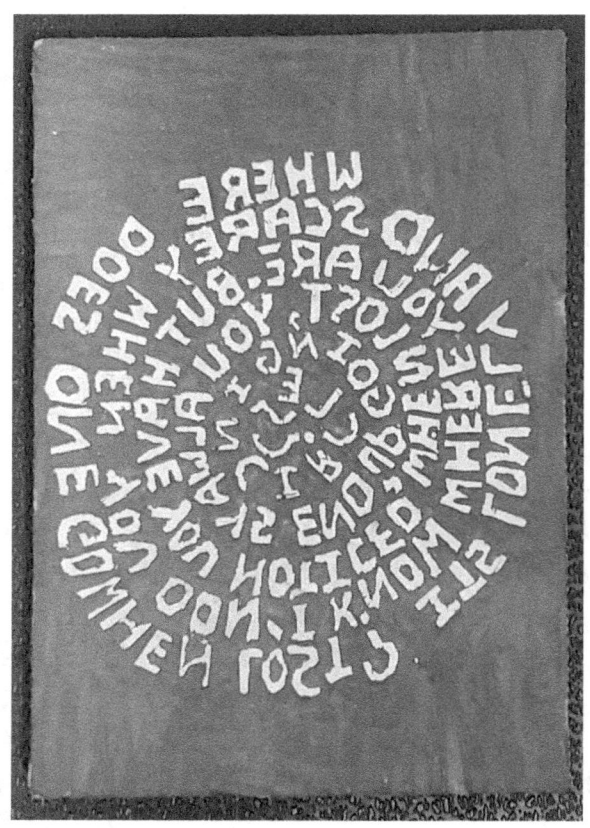

Other than a moment of mortification she had misspelled the word *scary* as *scarey*, I was immediately captivated by her wisdom and depth. In case mirror-reading isn't your thing, here's what her mind had spun:

WHERE DOES ONE GO WHEN LOST? IT'S LONELY AND SCAREY WHEN YOU DON'T KNOW WHERE YOU ARE. BUT HAVE YOU NOTICED, WHEN LOST, YOU ALWAYS END UP GOING IN CIRCLES?

How different life will be for future generations, as we each step into our assigned roles as trusted mentors and elders. Imagine encouraging creative expression for all. Let's be especially compassionate toward those who are convinced they have a huge rhombus but are being forced to compete against those who always appear perfectly shapely.

Fighting our natural flow, we get caught in a whirlpool of story. When we're circling the drain, we might believe our only choices are to give up or give in. But noticing concentric patterns resurfacing is the first cue: We are ready to halt our spiraling thoughts and behaviors.

Ah, if only I could go back in time, knowing what I do now. Well, there's no sense in continuing to tell myself that circular story. As an elder, it's my job to accept each life experience while empathizing with the part of me who prefers hiding out, doing what it has always done, because it doesn't yet know how to do it differently.

So here I am, doing something different: Expressing through my authentic heart, I am carving away at the synchronic mnemonics that kept me mired in a story that no longer serves. I am encircling perceived errors of the past with love, compassion, and forgiveness of self and others.

When you find yourself trudging along a route you vowed you'd never take again, remember: You haven't actually ended up where you started. There's always one traveling with you who is full of experience and self-compassion, ready to show itself to you in new forms. It circles back around, waiting for your reception, from a new perception.

How you treat yourself today is who you bring with you tomorrow.

You may as well make peace with your quirkiness. Gifts and talents cannot be lost. Listen for that wise, future-self whispering in your ear, gently reminding you that you'll always be in process, and that divine right direction always arrives, right on time.

Noticing the distraction, you asked what your blocks were. Just the willingness to ask and to receive gave you your answer. The act of asking brought awareness of the thoughts that were seemingly keeping you from connecting with Me. I didn't go anywhere, for *I AM* everywhere. Through the experience of checking in, as opposed to habitual checking out, the Voice is as clear as if I were right here with you. And *I AM*.

— *G.O.D. Journals, August 2012*

THE CIRCLE OF BLAME

Modus operandi works, until it doesn't.

When my modus stops operating, playtime becomes impossible. Circling the drain of familiar refrain signals that my default operating system is demanding an update—likely heading toward shutdown. Seen another way, perhaps my retention of the subject of my contention is here to inform me: Something must still be processing.

Self-righteously telling myself I don't know how to fix anything while refusing to ask for help hides my underlying fear: What if I break it, make it worse? Better keep doing the same old thing. Gather more information, until content overload forces me to crash.

Operating from a mode of conscientious contentiousness became my default approach to deal with my discontent toward others. Chronically embattled between a sincere desire to connect authentically while holding them in secret contempt, was, to be sure, disconcerting.

I still have no idea who or what possessed me one fateful Sunday.

Perhaps it was the excitement of being around like-minded folks on similar paths. Maybe I was unconsciously practicing living from my emerging spiritual self. Going with the flow, trusting my intuition, following my divine direction.

Or, more likely, too much caffeine.

When I heard myself invite our new acquaintances to join us on the beach that afternoon, right smack-dab in the middle of our sacred family vacation, I immediately felt betrayed. By me. Who the hell was this person inside, doing all the talking, and why wouldn't she shut up?

I suppose I unconsciously assumed these folks were just like me, and would never, ever accept a spur-of-the-moment invitation from someone they just met. Relationships have to build slowly, don't they? One must exercise caution, practice healthy boundaries. How did they not know that I was just being polite and didn't mean it?

Their immediate, overly enthusiastic, affirmative response should have been my first clue.

Thankfully, after decades of practice, I was fairly adept at kicking myself internally while covering my immediate remorse and subsequent distress. So, I did what I knew how to do: slap on my Sunday smile, secretly sigh, and accept what was nigh. We were having guests.

Acceptance. Awareness. A vague desire to lift my altitude, shift my attitude. How bad could it be? I was spiritually savvy enough to know we attract like-minded souls, and these folks were part of a well-respected, conscious, community. With a change of heart, I began to actually look forward to an afternoon of deep conversation, sharing, connection, and mutual healing with our new best friends.

Except. I also attract that which my shadow side prefers to hide.

As we settled on the sand, the conversation immediately turned to my trigger subjects. Obsession with food, bodies, weight, and diets. Sad childhoods, reiterating old hurts. They hated their jobs, their bosses. Endless stories of betrayal of family, friends, ex-spouses, cynical teenagers, aging parents. Everyone and everything were fair game for blame.

Always willing to be helpful, my subtle self-righteousness tried steering the conversation toward the spirituality, recovery, and self-responsibility genres I knew so well. Once again, I could hardly wait to start changing these people's lives, spouting my knowledge, compassion, and deep understanding.

But I couldn't get a word in edgewise. They already knew exactly who and what needed to change, and how. They vaguely understood they, too, had a part but weren't quite ready to do anything about it. After all, there was always tomorrow, and hopefully by then, someone else would do the changing.

Feeling left out, unseen, and definitely unheard, I did what I knew how to do. Go inside. Judge. Inwardly cringe while they discussed their over-the-top knowledge about nutrition while passing around bags of junk food. *People!* I screamed internally. *Just because the chip package says* VEGGIE *does not mean it is healthy!*

Clearly, they weren't just like me after all. Their strong opinions and victim mentality gave them an air of pretentiousness that was truly pissing me off. They had no desire to do their own recovery work! Couldn't they see their unhealthy thought patterns and behaviors, combined with refusal to take uncomfortable action, was leading them nowhere?

This is not a matter of withholding, blame, or even responsibility. Rather, it is a matter of willingness and acceptance of what is.

— *G.O.D. Journals, July 2014*

Bored out of my mind, I made a beeline for the ocean, baptizing myself in salt water, merging stinging, salty tears with emerging awareness. Overtaken by an unexpected wave of deep sadness, I was beholden to guilt. I got what I deserved. I had been the one to initiate, then facilitate, this theft of my energy. I'd been judging them. And, fervently wishing they would just leave.

Watching myself grieve the fact that, once again, I was beating myself up while wishing my life away, I gently comforted myself, acknowledging I just needed some alone time. Awareness, thankfully, had brought me back to the present, with an air of compassion for all. Making my way back to my towel, my reopened heart felt refreshed and relieved, secretly grateful in knowing the afternoon was soon coming to an end.

Until. Someone had the audacity to suggest we all go to dinner.

What choice did I have but to ignore my own impeding process, and agree that was a wonderful idea? Of course, they wanted to shower first. Awkward. Inner tension building, I resentfully watched bodies happily march up to our now very-crowded hotel room. And, of course, I had to politely offer up the hotel towels I had been carefully squirreling away. Thieves.

Incredibly irritated, resentful, and exhausted from pretending I wasn't irritated, resentful and exhausted, my mental and emotional victim was utterly attached to my stories about *them*. Yet part of me knew. It wasn't them at all. The *them* in me was being called forward.

I don't remember how the dinner went, I likely checked out by overeating. When the evening finally dragged to an end, it took all I had to muster up a masterful moment of false-falsetto cheeriness. "Thanks for joining us!" I lied.

As we said our goodbyes, they excitedly announced another wonderful idea! They'd call in sick to work the next day, so they could join us again tomorrow! *Really?!*

All I could do was what I knew how to do. Smiles, everybody, smiles.

As the door shut behind them, I took a deep breath. Embracing a moment of unexpected amusement, I randomly recalled an old *Saturday Night Live* bit entitled "The Thing That Wouldn't Leave." (Just found it on YouTube. It ends with the quip, "You may never have guests again.")

My secret mind has always been a good friend. It reminds me to keep things light, while remembering anything irritating me about *them* is just a reflection of me.

As was often the case in those days, rhyme, revenge, and relief insisted I had no need to sleep. So, I got back up, readied myself with pen and paper, and listened. I knew I was in training, and by then, by God, my G.O.D. had my attention, in a delightful way I no longer wanted to ignore.

Circle of Blame

I'm spinning in a circle of blame
Weary, though I'm winning the game
Since I know once you change
My life will rearrange
But for now, I'm spinning in a circle of blame

Been so depressed, can't get any rest
Hear my drama and I know you'll agree
Though the characters may shift
My excuse is always swift
You know who's at fault — and it's not me

Still spinning in this circle of blame
Exhausted, though controlling the game
Cause I'm sure once they change
My life will rearrange
So, I'll stay spinning in this circle of blame

Something feels a little less than light
Then I get a brief insight
And may even start — to go a little deep
But that means walking in the dark
And owning my own part
Never mind — besides, I'm sure I am right

Keep spinning in a circle of blame
Don't know where it's headed, where to aim
Yet, given they still could change
Not to mention it'd be awfully strange—to wonder . . .
Who could I be—without my circle of blame?

Though my victim role
Has really taken quite its toll
And this story—is finally boring—even me
Now I see no need for regret
Because suddenly—I so get
The turn—at the one hundred eightieth degree

It's time to leave my circle of blame
Energy's no longer the same
Found it was only me who had to change
Then nature somehow rearranged . . .

Wave goodbye to the circle of blame . . .
Farwell to the circle of blame . . .
Au revoir to the circle of blame . . .

Channeled Poetry, June 2004

CHAPTER 9

trying is trying

When things seem difficult, it's because you stopped. You think it's because you stopped doing your current *should*. Can you not see this is just an excuse to justify self-judgment? Next, you buy into the false idea that once you start doing the thing again, all will be well. But it's never about stopping or starting anything. That just gets your attention. In reality, what you first stopped doing was turning to Me. Your ongoing practice is to ask for Guidance from One Who Knows. Stop trying to protect your ego and start trusting your Self.

— *G.O.D. Journals, September 2014*

The idea of "trying" was irritating me.

You see, Dear Reader, I was simply trying to find a coherent way to express the value of listening to all our befuddled parts inside while desperately trying to ignore my own.

Unawareness, I suspect, prefers we get lost in the trials of trying to figure out solutions that have not yet revealed themselves, as opposed to lovingly accepting where we are.

When I don't know what to say or do, a foregone, woebegone conclusion is bound to follow: *This is too damn hard, takes too damn long, and I damn well quit.*

Sorry, this is the roughshod egoic show. Stop that whiny whinnying, and saddle up, pal!

Nay, trojan horse, neigh. Time to rein you in. You're racing down the wrong path. Chomping at the bit, you aren't stable. When you're trying too hard to win, you place against yourself.

Exacta.

Try again, Straight-A student.

Awareness understands that any ride of your life, especially one where you haven't yet been, will entail plodding through the mud, trotting and tripping over those unforeseen ruts in the road.

Meanwhile, Authenticity screams: *It's a dead end! I've been clip-clopping around this damn cul-de-sac of "I don't know what I'm doing" forever! This is going nowhere!*

Acceptance chimes in: *Aha! There it is.* Excellent! Your current "nowhere" brings you back, "now-here." Another breath bellows an additional authentic cry: *But I'm so damn tired of trying!*

Alignment empathizes. *I hear you. So, let's clip the clop clutter, kick it to the curb for the moment, and reaffirm: We are committed.*

Asking for assistance, my next action humbly presented itself. *HELP!*

How about you go inside and listen? You are trying too hard. You keep trying to figure things out without My help. Get present in your body again. Go back to what you were doing before you started overthinking. Let Me show you. Be willing to wait. You don't have to, nor can you, do this alone.

— *In the Moment G.O.D.*

Relief. I've been heard.

Trying *is* trying. Trying to figure out how to do what I've never done, trying to control, trying to be witty, trying to sound perfectly brilliant. Hell, even synonyms for *trying* sound exhausting: struggling, irritating, annoying, demanding, exasperating, taxing. *Ugh.* Yet sitting in the waiting room of not-knowing seems even more trying than expending the energy to keep on trying the same old tired thoughts and ways of being I already know won't work.

See what I mean? Even this discussion around the word *trying* is trying.

We get oh-so-tired when we try oh-so-hard. Just thinking about how hard you've tried can make you tired, it's true. Hey, maybe the word *and* in the phrase *tried and true* is a pause worth noting. We've tried *everything* (so we told ourselves, though that can't possibly be true). But in context, isn't everything true—meaning at some level it somehow contributed to your growth? Imagine accepting trials and triggers as quasi-pieces in the quest for peace.

Yeah, sure. Imagine that. The hard reality is, sometimes life is hard.

But maybe hard reality isn't hard at all. Life is pliable. Perceived *reality* shifts every instant. Our interpretation of this millisecond belongs only to this millisecond. We can either accept the momentary feedback we are receiving or go to battle with it. Which feels more peaceful? Hmm.

Perhaps the difficulty only lies in surrendering to what is. Creator or reactor, our choice awaits.

Trying to stop being your Self is what exhausts you. While waiting to get inspired, you are listening with the ears of the ego. I tell you anyone who is willing can tune in and hear My Voice. There is nothing special about it. Notice how trying seems to elude your Direction, pulling you right back into resistance.

— *G.O.D. Journals, June 2012*

TAKING TRYING OFF OF TRIAL

Ah, verbs. Action words, ways of being.

Being a character witness for our shadow requires enlightening-up prior to summoning-up enough courage to serve up a subpoena or two. Telling ourselves the truth, the whole truth, and nothing but the truth isn't easy, especially when, according to my judgment—you know, always by the book here—there surely must be an inner liar (lawyer) lurking about, determined to enrich itself through intimidating those of us who prefer to stand for authenticity.

The liar's only stipulation is to keep us upset. Arguing for shame and blame, its game is to victimize the victim. Its oath of allegiance is in persistently presenting well-prepared evidence, reprovingly re-proving life is a perpetual problem. Forever focused on the nonexistent past or future, its justification of *trying* is designed to keep us on trial.

When I find myself humbly mumbling "I'm trying," what I'm really trying to do is duck interrogation by the world's harshest attorney: me. Talk about a cross-examination. Every minute, every minute detail is being crankily dissected by my inner alligator-litigator. Going by the book, it tears every sentence apart, affirming nothing is right. No sense in trying to file a demand for requital (to meekly plead for acquittal) since the underlying message is quite clear: *quit!*

Bah, justice! Verdict's in. Perpetual trying shall be followed by perpetual crying. Guilty as charged. Case dismissed. So much for free trials. There's always a catch.

But wait—there's more!

Quasi-quitting quickly quashes quiet, quality questioning. Since inspired inquisitiveness invokes important information, be sure to take a moment to question the quality of your questioning. Who or what *makes you* think you shouldn't be exactly where you are, in body, mind, spirit? Catching yourself perpetuating an illusion that you should, somehow, already know what you don't, be somewhere you aren't, feel something you can't, or complete something you haven't, is powerful feedback.

Stop the perjury! Per the jury, all witnesses must be heard!

What goes on during those secret sidebar conversations? And who are all those so-called expert witnesses? Maybe know-it-alls don't know it all. Where's the reasonable doubt here? The people have a right to know! Don't the most frightened parts of ourselves deserve their long-awaited day in court too?

NO NEED TO LOATH THE OATH

Summoning up my courage, I shall raise my right hand and declare my moment of truth. Subject to change, of course, since it's only this moment's perception of what I fear is true.

> *"I'm trying, I really am!"*
>
> *Translated: "I don't know how I landed here again, caught in this guilt-gilded cage. I'm winging it. Can't fly the coop and can't chicken out. I'm either going to be booted out of the nest or trapped here forever. Truth is, I'm afraid to fly."*
>
> *To the rescue! My inner wise owl swoops in. "Take a time of respite. Remember your early training. You need not completely ground yourself, nor be flighty on this turbulent journey. Yet rest and reset are required safety precautions prior to takeoff."*
>
> *Wow. Maybe my flock of inner fowls' foul moves are trying to soar to new heights.*

Surrender may be reluctant at first, but let's courageously call forth our inner witnesses. Maybe it's time to stop justifying the justifications that keep us stuck in an unconscious victim position. The more we free ourselves from self-judgment, the more we recuse (rescue?) ourselves from holding onto a collective guilty mindset. How frequently and mercilessly we've put ourselves and others on trial! Walking around in self-defense, it's no wonder life seemed so trying.

I'm having a *duh* moment here. Prejudice results from prejudgment.

Perhaps the only fact of the matter is the only fact that matters: We all seek peace of mind. Doesn't our Declaration of Innocence clearly state we must treat all as the guiltless beings we all are? Imagine this updated courtroom scenario:

The hearing begins with "All Rise," affirming all are called to rise to their higher purpose. Every soul's sole role is to silently attune to Wise Inner Council. Gently witnessing each witness, with openminded, heart-centered, neutral observation, inner jurors remain fully present. Their silent, yet compassionate, consciousness creates space for honest, heartfelt sharing, reaffirming the power of self-forgiveness. Your Honor, the wisdom of the higher court reigns. Trials and tribulations transformed; transcendence prevails.

Hear ye, hear ye! It is time for Truth to preside.

Forgive yourself and others for any past error in judgment. Gift yourself a guilt-free mindset as you join in the quest for inner freedom. Be willing to ask for, and receive, the very Guidance that wants nothing more than to reveal Itself to you.

You know, just try it.

This is an adventure in trust. Let the Source that created you guide the way. You can hear My Voice—when you stop trying. Trying only distracts you. Instead, relax into the experience and watch it happen. Would you not prefer a world of Guided Omnipresent Direction?

— *G.O.D. Journals, May 2017*

THE WONDERFUL THING ABOUT TRIGGERS

So, let's talk about triggers, shall we?

"No," you say. "It triggers me too much."

I hear you. You have good reason to stay pissed. But who suffers?

Ever find yourself faithfully reciting, "lead me not into temptation" as temptation leads you right back into excuses to stay upset? Great. Just let that be where it is, and join me in a good rant, will you? Who or what are your go-to triggers? Don't worry, I'll start.

People, places, things. Situations. Opinions. Weather. Clutter. Noise. Thoughts. Emotions. Words. Typos. Behaviors. Mirrors. Traffic. Inconvenient bodily needs and associated audio-visuals; breathing and chewing in particular. Stuff that breaks. Food. Religion. Politics. Smells. Need I continue? Yes.

What about know-it-alls who clearly know nothing? What about all these damn people in my way, audaciously assuming their agenda and timeline is more important than mine? What about over-explainers who detail everything to death? And what about those who cite endless what-about-isms instead of doing their own inner work? Pretentious projectors, all of them.

Deep breath. A little mist to polish the mirror.

A friend recently shared a preference for the term *activator* over *trigger*. A call to action.

Admiration or admonition, observing who or what activates your reactions might just be a powerful step in determining your next indicated action.

To transcendence, and beyond.

Triggers are often followed by an almost insatiable desire to hide, condemn, or perform. Yet the Higher Self knows there is nothing to fix—only opportunities

166

to learn to be more loving with yourself, others, the situation.

— *G.O.D. Journals, March 2012*

I find *Winnie the Pooh* characters particularly endearing— cleverly representative of unique aspects within our shared human experience. Compulsion, caution, wisdom, joy. Depression. Playfulness. Each of our components, though sometimes competitive, contains essential contributions to our overall story. No lesson need be lessened; no portion of our personas need be pooh-poohed.

Inner Pooh is, predominantly, a cheerful, patient, and gentle soul. Catching a glimpse of how we look in too-tight pants may be only mildly bothersome, until we find ourselves stuck in a hole of despair, perhaps due to last night's honey binge. Suddenly, all our troubles seem magnified, becoming almost too much for dear inner bear to bear.

Inner Rabbit nervously fusses, trying oh-so-hard to pre-fix potential problems, while plucky, perceptive, precious Inner Piglet quiets inner panic, utilizing well-practiced codependency. Inner mother Kanga gently offers calm, loving encouragement, ensuring her baby Roo and all his friends feel safe and loved, while Inner Owl wisely encourages thought intervention through closed-eye meditation. I mostly rally around Inner Eeyore, whose momentum for momentous moments of meaningful melancholy is measureless.

Oh, bother! Just what we need. Here comes Inner Tigger, happily bouncing in the sunshine, while the rest of us are busy ruminating in our varied remediation roles. Trigger time!

Well-meaning intentions aren't always aligned with one's current experience. Trying to play when you're not feeling it can be totally trying. Leaving the pity pot before we're done dumping can land us right back in the honeypot, stuck in a sticky mess of disingenuity.

Triggers are unprocessed hurts. So, when I'm triggered, the work is mine. Damn it. I don't want to work. But for the sake of goodness, I suppose I could compromise with Tigger and at least try to have a bit of fun. A vacillation vacation, veering between being sensible while remaining incensed.

Awareness of current authenticity is agonizing when acceptance isn't present. Yet.

With focus realigned, I can ask my inner guidance counselor to help create an elective course of action. I know — we'll combine triggers, trying, shapes, and numbers into one advanced class, and call this blockbuster learning opportunity "Trigger-Not-Me-Try." Once I ace that trigonometrical teaching, for sure, I'll never be triggered again, right?

Booyah! Pomp that circumstance!

On another (musical) note, my inner child has always been fond of musicals. Loving the magical, miraculous, and mysterious, she delighted in watching how main characters always managed, just in the nick of time, to channel the perfect melodies and lyrics; effortlessly singing and dancing their way right through challenges. Maybe they were onto something. So, let's try to face our triggers in a similar way!

If you happen to know the tune of the signature song belonging to Disney's take on A. A. Milne's most joyful tiger-like character, please, sing along! Together, we'll work through the trials of triggers, utilizing a creative — you know, versus reactive — set of alternative lyrics:

> *The wonderful thing about triggers*
> *Is triggers are wonderful things!*
> *Their stories make me suffer*

And these thoughts
Oh, how they sting!

Ignoring, storing, boring story
No longer fun, fun, fun, fun, fun
There's no one here to fix me!
Since I'm the only one!
Yeah, damn it, I'm the only one.

Judgments, distractions, musings all reside out there—in the head, away from Higher Mind. Nothing is wrong, it's only exactly that—nothing. Stop trying. This is from your ego. Physically move your energy as you imagine moving from your head to your heart. Focus on your heart and flow from there. Your Direction is to follow your Direction, without attachment to any particular outcome.

— *G.O.D. Journals, June 2012*

When triggers make your mind bounce, invite stuck energy to come forward. Get up and give your mind, voice, and body permission to express themselves in any funky way they choose. Be amused as your bemused muse plays right out in front of you. It might just surprise and delight you. Where do creative moments come from, anyway?

Consider your most beloved artists, authors, mentors, musicians, poets, philosophers. You are in awe of them precisely because they risked bringing their creator-self into being. What may have started as their trigger somehow morphed into tangible energy that became their form of expression, which eventually inspired you. What if they had refused to listen to the Direction that prompted them to share *their* heart? You wouldn't ever have had the pleasure of receiving the great gift they have given you.

Why would it be any different for you? You, too, are here to give, in the way only you can.

Acknowledge the part of you who recognizes yourself in that annoying other. Whether you are jealous or judging, connection with projection gives your friend Trigger permission to delight in your secret desire to stop fighting what is.

Might you be ready to acknowledge that maybe, just maybe, your triggers aren't against you after all? Allow your inciters to grant your insight. See your circumstance as your meant-to-happenstance. See the error in terror. Enlighten up, and stop waiting to be peaceful.

Triggered by this discussion? Me too. Still, Tigger always bounces back, and so do you.

Child, you keep wanting to make this part of your process, but not that. You can substitute in any this or that you want, so you can remain in your judgment, your assessment of matters. Or you can leave matters to Me. Let Me discern what the matter actually is: What matters, what doesn't. Every experience is meant to enhance your life experience, used for the Higher Good. Stay on track. Listening right now is tracking with Me. That is always your best use of time.

— *G.O.D. Journals, January 2021*

ABANDON SHIT!

In the past, self-abandonment may have seemed like your only viable route.

Except, it never really is. You're still here, aren't you? You didn't lose yourself after all.

Likewise, dodging the crap we'd prefer not to deal with doesn't necessarily make it disappear. Perhaps it's inevitable that we cannot permanently put off that which is inevitable.

If you notice Captain Sabotage queuing up for a long retreat on Incapability Island, maybe that's your no-fault signal to give up remorse and change course. Even irrationality can appear rational when we remain unaware of its anchor in the past, so riding those waves of awareness may require taking a deeper dive.

Releasing reproach creates space for a new approach. Use your curiosity to pump up your velocity as you uncover new bits o' shift. Who inside yourself were you tempting to abandon, and who in you was doing the abandoning? Terrified of the unknown, we become captivated by our inner captives. Incessant desires to please may conceal a backlog of pleas for reassurance, triggering more behaviors that aren't particularly pleasing.

Ever take a head trip to nowhere? The depths of imagination are unimaginable. Originality originates from within, leading me to wonder, from where did originality originally originate?

Always in the process of arrival, we'll never know the outcome of a chosen action until we choose it and actually do it. "But I don't know what's going to happen!" you cry. *Duh.* But you do know, from experience, excess spinning in a whirlpool of worthlessness is bound to make you sick. Unconscious attachments to defenses prevent natural flow, dam it all.

I'm certain current stream-of-consciousness is always overflowing with visual value and metaphoric meaning. What's up? Tuning in. Listening.

> If you're *shoulding* on yourself, wouldn't that automatically define you as a *shoulder*? Your *shoulds* are hard on your shoulders. Putting more burden on those already-burdened shoulders of yours has a predictable ending: Everyone and everything will become a pain in your neck.
>
> — *In the Moment G.O.D.*

Okay, then. And ouch.

Noticing my downright defiance and codependent compliance, I'm beginning to realize even resistance need not be resisted. Halting that head trip to nowhere, however, does require awareness. Hearing myself indulge in innuendoes while retelling tired old tales serves as an embarrassing reminder that I just might be in recreational denial; unwittingly luxuriating in recreating contributions to the next chapter in my heretofore unlived story.

Thankfully, though, habitual responses don't necessarily insist on immediate change. Prompts to pause are simply momentary invitations back to present awareness. The choice for choosing a more authentic, aligned action is only a decision away.

Isn't every conscious decision simply an opportunity to increase awareness while practicing taking dominion over a previously unconscious mind? You can always decide to accept you aren't ready to decide because, done consciously, you have, indeed, made a decision. It's okay to wait for alignment as you summon the courage to ask for help before taking that courageous next action.

Every decision will have an outcome, followed by an opportunity to make another choice. Kinda takes the pressure off, right?

Reinterpret I don't know as wait or listen more closely. The message, the higher knowing, for this Now moment is always here. Knowing you do not know, or need not yet know, helps you remember there is a Part inside that does. Wait for the Still Small Voice in the silence. Listen for the Gentle Voice of Peace.

— *G.O.D. Journals, December 2015*

STOP TRYING TO FIGURE IT OUT

Perfectionism precedes procrastination.

I sense awareness glaring at me as I attempt to ignore the agony of the hour.

Frustrated at the futility of trying to figure out exactly how to articulate the futility of trying to figure anything out, I'm rapidly tiring of trying. Besides, all my triggers are tripping.

No wonder I've learned to love my *Later*.

Predictability prevails. Dismissing the discomfort available in momentary authenticity will likely result in incomplete insight, tossing me out of my body, right into self-judgment. Next, the magical wave of the hand will appear. "Never mind. I'll figure it out—*later*." Never mind, indeed. It's no fun minding the disgruntled mutterings of the disgusted mind.

Could it be that *figuring it out* rests on the very foundation of futility; attempts to think about that which actually must be felt? When I'm busy wasting time avoiding acceptance of whatever emotion is authentically present, chances are I'm giving Ms. Judgment the power to block me from my God-given right to be both human and a divine creation.

Proceed with caution. An avalanche of inappropriateness is likely imminent when I finally face the fact that I have no clue as to what to do.

The saying, "You can't think your way into a right way of acting but can act your way into a right way of thinking," just came to mind.

Perhaps I had good reason to defend my heart by staying in my head. Arresting authenticity is an automatic reaction when I fear facing my own thoughts, emotions, and actions. Then there's facing the risk of sharing them with others, or, for that matter, remembering that "alone" can always be reinterpreted as "all-one."

Imagine retraining our minds and hearts to trust and accept that which is authentically present. Unafraid of engaging with the quiet, we notice gentle inner encouragement to engage with our momentary disquiet. The mind, the heart, the body—all here; all one, for us to hear.

Hmm. Sensing some phantasmic phantoms lurking about.

Aha! There you are. Inadequacy. Impatience. Imprisonment. Fearing conviction by others, every sentence I write compounds the deeper fear of taking responsibility and owning the possibility I'm only a convict of my own convictions.

I'm tired of trying to figure out how to escape from this incessant insecurity that Help will never arrive.

Because somehow, It always does.

Mind Captive

Distractions from the outside world
Are lost between these walls
No everyday diversions here
No theaters or malls

Heart is feeling heavy
Mind is full of fear
From myself I crave escape
God, let me outta here

Nowhere safe to let it go
Yet no place left to hide
Holding tight onto this anger, though
Seems somehow justified

Self-righteousness I lug around
Oblivious as to what it weighs
Useless phrases precede my thoughts ~
"If only"s "What if"s and "They"s

Judgment keeps the heart shut down
Defensive, ready for fight
Allowing this bitter darkness
To shadow God's healing light

Yet in brief moments of awakening
And in the silence do I see
Freedom is right here and now
When I connect to God in me

Creator, grant me willingness
To open the prison of my mind
Release these thoughts that hurt so much
And reveal the truth of Who I'll find

Channeled Poetry, August 2002

The insanity of trying to figure out what to do is an attempt to control, to scare, yourself. You need not figure out anything in advance. You have NO IDEA what is unfolding. Let Me witness your fears as they arise, so they are seen, but not retained. Only then can I retrain you in your job, to remain presently in love, which requires constant, conscious rejoining with Me.

— *G.O.D. Journals, June 2020*

CHAPTER 10

overwhelmers anonymous

You tend to overthink things, making them big in your mind. You overwhelm yourself, adding to your own misery. Child, do you not understand you have only this moment, right here, now, with Me? Take a deep breath. Instead of losing your Self in a mind maze of imaginings, of a literally nonexistent past or future, be amazed at the Presence available in this moment.

— G.O.D. Journals, July 2021

OVERWHELM OVERVIEW

Do you create your own chaos, making things harder on yourself? Do you feel frustrated when the nouns you are trying to control don't cooperate? Do guilty feelings concerning lack of focus keep you from focusing? Do you keep trying to fix things that aren't broken? Are you irritated by interruptions? Do you feel responsible when you aren't? Do you avoid actions you know you ought to take, or take actions you know you ought to avoid? *Are you annoyed by annoying questioners who ask annoying questions?*

Welcome to Overwhelmers Anonymous. If you regularly experience feelings of over-and underwhelm, you just might be in the right chapter. Swamped or stumped, amidst the dance of drama, perhaps you, too, share the dilemma of trying to look like you have your shit together, particularly when you don't.

Case in point: Diversion calls, I answer.

Is whelm its own word? Ah, apparently so, and entertainingly, a synonym for overwhelm itself! Double trouble! Right-clicking on whelm *further suggests* overtake *and* sweep over *as viable options. Oddly, as lack of focus begins to overpower, I hear my new friend, Whelm, whispering, "Take a peek. What are you sweeping under that lovely rug of yours?"*

Okay. Weird. Breathe. Pause. Peek.

While pouring energy into insistent thoughts that writing a book is overwhelmingly overpowering, I've forgotten I'm not my own Higher Power. When I decide that I, alone, must decide how to immediately resolve that which I've decided needs immediate resolution, I've ensured my own overwhelm. Refusing to ask for help, I foolishly conclude that steeping in seething is somehow less overwhelming than soaking in a spa of surrender.

Overwhelm equals taking over. But where does it come from?

"I don't know!" you exclaim. "Just make it stop!"

But who is "it"? Who or what has the power to make it stop, when endless entities (those nouns, thoughts, and emotions) keep finding new ways to hold you hostage?

Let's face it, it's no fun feeling buried alive. Especially when you are the one who has been doing most of the digging.

Let go of the guilt. You didn't mean to hurt yourself.

I know you think it's hard to surrender to Me. Life circumstances seem overwhelming and impossible. What if this were an opportunity for a breakthrough? What part of you is picking up the pen, allowing My Voice to flow through your thoughts, through your hand, and onto paper? Do you feel the rise in energy? Notice how the rest of it (the to-dos, the stories, the feelings, the overwhelm) simply dissolves when you do. I know you like your stories, but they are wearing you out. That's why this feels so big right now. But don't stop. This isn't the time for quitting, distraction, or limiting thoughts. Just don't do anything today without conscious awareness of Me. Keep practicing. See what happens.

— *G.O.D. Journals, February 2012*

HURRICANE JANITOR

When incongruent intentions permeate thoughts, they tend to offer generous contributions toward an ever-increasing sense of overwhelm. Life events have a way of presenting themselves long before we are ready.

Mindlessly allowing thoughts to race their way right back into today's destruction derby is likely to impede any intended outcome—or implode against it. If that which you try to outrun typically ends in crash-and-burn, it's time to consider thoughtfully slowing down.

The mind often seems as if it has a mind of its own, overtaking our more mindful agenda. Subtly at first, it goes its merry way, unnoticed, unchecked, running amok for hours, days, years, decades. With fear as its frontrunner, it's easy to ignore the fact that we have to stop running away from it long enough for it to stop running us.

If you've been living full speed ahead of yourself, put on your brakes, and take a break.

There's an infamous persona who lives in me I've dubbed the *Hurricane Janitor*. An oblivious obliterator, it gets powered by my inner cyclonic activity; often sighted during an overwhelm cycle. Fueled by fear and fury, it's a whirlwind of swirling ideas, regrets, and control, sucking anything nearby into its tornadic temper tantrum, sans any care, clue, or concern about the mess it must invariably leave behind.

Science or celestial safety nets, spinning thoughts can actually propel us upward into awareness. Even resentment, rumination, and repudiation deserve reconsideration. Although likely unnoticed until the downward spiral, calm does eventually follow a storm. Whatever is in our path will lead us where we need to go, once we decide to follow it.

It's wise to regularly check in. See who's minding the mind. Ask a few gentle questions. *What are you running from? What are you racing toward?* As you listen for authentic answers, imagine every aspect of your mind as a revered tag-team member, each in their unique way cheering you on while aligning with your most heartfelt aspirations.

There is no need to get caught up in drama. Enjoy watching the play, but stop pretending you are something you are not. It's called "play" because the drama isn't real. If you are experiencing anything other than profound love for everyone and everything, keep in mind there is a happy ending on the way.

— *G.O.D. Journals, June 2015*

INFORMATION JUNKIES

Who here secretly values information over transformation? *As soon as I get just a little more info, I'll act in a new way,* we tell ourselves. *I'm just not quite ready yet.* Funny how overthinking leads to thoughtlessness. Contemplation becomes complicated. Musing, snoozing. You know overanalyzing is paralyzing. We defend ourselves from the fear we all hear, yet an overwhelming voice reigns, both clear and severe: *Don't you dare make a mistake!*

Who is that inside, anyway? What's it afraid of? As you consider all the possibilities, it's possible overthinking will lead you right back into overwhelm.

Stop! Shh! I need to stop thinking about how to stop thinking! Ever wish everyone would just shut their piehole? Oh, and watch yourself the next time you chatter nervously, embarrassingly unable to stop, then overcompensate, delivering a prolonged silent treatment.

Apparently, the universe needed to call me out, as a friend recently shared an amusing acronym:

WAIT = Why Am I Talking?

Pause your pattern by minding your mind, and your mouth. Breathe in your Guidance, allowing Essential Self to work through you. Invite your information system to become your transformation system. Stop giving your power away by gently owning your own stuff. Guess who I'm talking to?

There it is again. That precarious, punitive perspective that persistently insists I am too much or not enough. Designed to throw me off-balance, maybe it's time I rebel. I wonder if letting go of both my tight-ass attitude and this ongoing tightrope act would achieve just a moment's equilibrium? Hell, what's a little fall from grace?

No noun has the power to *make you* feel or do anything. When stress starts stressing, how does *your* inner manager typically manage? Like me, you might over- or under-eat, -sleep, -exercise; over- or under-spend time, money, resources. Chronically late or staying too long, you may overpower others while continuing to undermine yourself.

Don't overthink this, but before over- or under-whelm takes over, what might change if you became aware of your overthinking sooner? Imagine giving that meathead mindset a rest. Have a little fun while considering some juicy puns and meat-a-phors! Cut loose those choice beefs about others that you've been serving! Season them with a salty attitude and a peppered possibility of forgiveness. Marinate in that number one A.1. Sauce we keep pounding a stake in: Awareness.

Entertainingly, we humans spend a lot of time telling ourselves stories about how we ought to act while outright avoiding it. Becoming quickly incensed by our own insensibilities, we are stupefied right into inaction, and as a result, stupidly forget a simple-minded solution: When a particular action doesn't provide a desired result, take a different action. Easy, right? Sure.

Don't worry; it's normal to worry that whatever action you are thinking about thinking about maybe taking in the future will probably be the wrong one. So what?

Moreover, maybe what we need to do is move over. Give ourselves a little space, a moment of grace. My favorite dinosaur, Thesaurus, advises there are many more overs, indicating endless opportunity for do-overs. No wonder overwhelm gets so damn overwhelming.

Waiting for inspiration requires quieting the mind. Do you truly want inspiration? Then become willing to let go of your ego's motivations for recognition. Inspiration and life happen in the present. Let go of your plans and your agenda, allowing Me to show you through My Loving. Be a divine demonstrator. Becoming willing to wait, taking a moment—this moment—to ask, listen, and be silently inspired by Me. Trust My Guidance.

— G.O.D. Journals, August 2019

NO SENSE IN AGAINST

Notice the word *against* starts with *again*. Despite the affect of past effects, continuing to choose ineffective ways of being sabotages growth. When unaware of our omnipresent loving energy, bullying ourselves becomes a viable, albeit odd, option. Now, on top of our other stressors, we must defend ourselves—against ourselves.

Can you feel the anxiety of angst that's found in being against oneself or another? It's a fuel that feeds futility. Working against your natural life force of loving recreation is almost sure to result in a whole lot of extra work—for a whole lot of extra nothing.

Resentment adds to overwhelm, so shall we look instead? Who is the bully inside who attempts to bullshit or bulldoze you, and which part of you is it against? Which persona allows the unacceptable, then gets paid, perhaps in a type of familiar script-o-currency, for keeping its victim role? Who perpetrates? Who perpetuates? Who inside is observing all the resulting overwhelm?

Again and again, pause. Notice once again, for a-gain in perspective.

Attune to your awareness, authenticity, and acceptance. Check in with your alignment. If thoughts are delivering mostly angst, ask for a change in couriers, one aligned with the action of bringing messages you can use. Your deliverance depends upon your willingness to receive, then deliver, the divine messages you are directed to give.

There is nothing to fix, only opportunities to raise awareness. The cost of overwhelm equates to no time for re-creation. With so much on your "gotta do" list, you put off the very practices that nurture you, the ones that bring your awareness back to Me. Become present to the internal and external rushing. Show yourself the benefits of slowing down. You have all the time and support you need.

— *G.O.D. Journals, March 2012*

STRATA-GENIUS GAMES

Decades ago, I saw a sign in a dental office that read:

IGNORE YOUR TEETH, AND THEY'LL GO AWAY.

Considering wordplay's impact on both wisdom and teeth, even dental procedures leave useful, lasting, impressions. What we choose to ignore today might very well be rooted in tomorrow's pain and overwhelm.

Your habitual strategies are no mystery to your inner genius. To avoid stints into strenuous stupefaction, accept your inner challenger's request for a rousing game of Truth or Dare while invoking a little more awareness and authenticity.

Which tasks seem so off-putting that you must keep putting them off into an unforeseeable future that never arrives? What must happen before your inner knowing becomes so intolerably obvious that even the universe is tiring of thinking up new ways to awaken you from your not-so-blissful oblivion? Who in you continues to wait for *the* message, the one that will finally convince you to answer your call? Where, what, and with whom have you dared not play (or face) your own Truth-or-Consequences?

Bored with your current board position? *Wham-o!* It's time to play pun-fun! Who will win the honor of deciding when your life will become your Ideal Game? Will it be Milton, Bradley, one of the Parker Brothers, or the other wildcard bro, Hasbro?

It's time to get a Clue. Remember, you are the one who holds the Monopoly in this Operation. Let go of the competition and practice a little Stratego (strategizing with other egos), devising new ways to have fun while engaging with fellow players. Land for a moment in Candy Land, tasting the sweetness of all the Shenanigans, Charades, and Mousetraps your Game of Life is sure to bring.

Discover which of your stringent rules need to be updated, changed, broken, or tossed out entirely. But do so with integrity. No fair cheating anyone, including yourself, out of an opportunity for an amazing new win.

Whichever games you play, be they know-it-all or know-I-stall, any lack of tangible results is, well, a tangible result. The hardest part about getting started is getting started. The lower mind is brilliant at convincing itself its rationales are logical. But it really can't mess with the part of your mind that knows you'll never finish a project you won't start.

It's okay to dream and visualize, but stay present so you can hear Me. Often fantasy is simply mind-wandering, subtly substituting for mindfulness. Check in frequently, ensuring that you still hear the Still Small Voice within.

— *G.O.D. Journals, May 2019*

BEATING THE BEATEN PATH

Getting started on this overwhelming chapter was this procrastinator's dream, sliding right into my nightmare: The sloppy sideways segue onto the beat-me-up path.

Surely all I've written so far is crap. Overwhelm to the rescue. Here only to add to itself, it is insisting I accept my punishment: Start over, even though I know it still won't be right.

But wait. What if overwhelm is simply an irrational pain pile of the past? Perhaps practicing questioning the bottom line—that fear that somehow, I'm/they/it is not good enough—could provide a different answer.

In this neutral moment of moot, it occurs to me that *starting over* could be defined in a new context. Enchanted by possibility, I could indeed start over by changing my thinking path. Why not play with the word *START* instead? Who in me wouldn't love accepting a co-creative challenge; an acronymic way to get my ass in gear?

> S – STOP. Notice the upset. Observe, without reaction, those overwhelming voices inside.
>
> T – THINK about the direction the lower mind is headed. Must it be followed? Says who?
>
> A – ASK Higher Mind for Direction while acknowledging this practice moment.
>
> R – RE-MIND, literally. Choose Higher Mind over lower mind's overwhelming angst.
>
> T – TRUST in the Direction being received, bringing with it joy, humor, peace, serenity.

You are listening. Problem is, you are also judging your awarenesses. You deserve to live a life that is focused not only on what brings you joy but also brings joy to others. Imagine taking on demonstrating that, in the precise way you do very well? How many geniuses—that's everyone, in their own right-mind—hold themselves back from their calling, because they fear disapproval? And who decides to move forward anyway? The game-changers are the ones who say yes. Ready to play?

— *G.O.D. Journals, September 2014*

RAISE YOUR PINK FLAG!

Red flag warnings are here to inform. With our well-being in mind, their vivid color is designed to grab attention, ensuring we see, hear, and heed their caring message: *Caution!* Dangerous conditions may be looming.

But when it comes to potentially risky relationships or hazardous habits, how are foibles suddenly forgotten? Our inner red flags become a source of irritation and annoyance, something to ignore. In a way, though, forestalling makes sense, especially when used for stalling.

So, for what are we waiting? A redder flag?

As a wannabe artist and metaphor maniac, I wonder what might happen if we added a few muted colors to our flag palette, perhaps gifting us an ability to admire the lighter signs along the way. Imagine delighting in those oh-so-innocent, pinkish flags. You've seen them, right? Unobtrusively waving in the breeze, a calm invitation to consider taking a broader perspective.

Consider the adventures of Ms. Taken. Everything was smooth sailing until they began to ignore the subtle swelling of what ended up being not so swell.

Hey! Did anyone else notice those weird clouds gathering in the distance?

Always on the lookout for a waiver to wave away that which one prefers to overlook, those gently waving pretty pink flags can often go unacknowledged, or perhaps seen only as obstruction, spoiling the view of what one hopes is on the horizon.

Oh, wow, check out those crazy, amazing clouds! They're shaped like unicorns! Must be a sign from the Universe!

Ah, the drift of denial! Certainly, we've all disregarded those initial celestial signs; those early-warning signals, telling us we are beginning to coast toward a shore we'd rather not go. Yet the rebel rules. *Not ready! Can't make me!*

Sadly mistaking the orangish flag's supportive intention to grab their attention, Ms. Taken defiantly sails ahead, gaining headway while disregarding an inkling of quieter thinking: that maybe there is a CAUTION sign a' blinking.

Hey, no judgment. We just can't see what we aren't ready to see.

Attracted to a crew who unconsciously carried a voracious taste for victim drama, maybe Ms. Taken hadn't yet learned how to be on the observation deck, taking things piecemeal, bite by bite, which required savoring the unsavory. Understandable. Most of us have had to go through storms to see where we've been taken, and, very possibly, mistaken.

Um, anyone else noticing those flags seem to be morphing? Is it just me, or does it look like they just got a little darker? Even my crew is beginning to look and sound a bit concerned, but I'm not sure I understand why. Personally, I really love those warm salmon and coral shades! Besides, it's probably just the shadow of the setting sun.

They'll lighten up again tomorrow, right? At least I hope so.

Translated: That banner's bellowing manifesto is beginning to dawn on me: *Proceed with caution! Stop and think! Better still, don't proceed at all!* But that's no fun.

Hmm. The breeze is picking up. Crimson-colored flags are whipping around what used to be my safe harbor. The scents are a bit more pungent. Is it my briny brain, or is something fishy going on? Ooh! Check out that a-*lure*-ing bait over there! Did you notice? That one isn't just a shiny object—it has a lovely orange marshmallow attached!

I desperately deny what I know that I know: If I bite, I'll surely get entangled again. And hooked. But maybe not, since this time, I'm paying attention. I'm sure the outcome will be different.

Yes. For sure. This time, the outcome will be different.

Out of nowhere, the hurricane hits! Holy crap! Where the hell did all those flags come from, and when did they morph into that maniacal maroon? Oh man, wait! Is that my bleeding heart?

Resignation reigns when flags fly. Their partner poles pierce everywhere from betwixt the brows to up one's brutally bruised butt. Despite the deafening dread of shameful doom, an empathetic voice insists on taking the reins, speaking only gentle truth: *Baby, this is gonna hurt.*

I guess those stupid flags and their whole staff found a way to capture my awareness.

Shit. Wish I had paid attention sooner.

Gradients of our shadows teach us. Pink, salmon, red—no matter. Simply observing the presence of any flag is a great first step, so honor them when they wave. See their post, their stance, as your guidepost for strength.

Flow with what's current. Consider sailing in new directions. Sooner—or schooner, as the case might be—or later, whether you choose to salute them or not, you might notice a common theme in your flags' messages: Your inner freedom is up to you.

And if you notice yourself sinking, maybe this time, it won't be quite so deep.

In the interim, your job is to learn to sink responsibly.

Let everything be a reminder to tune in to My peace. You are becoming less tolerant of stress. This is progress—and opportunity. Instead of following stressful thoughts into the past or the future, ask for My peace in this moment. Let your challenging emotions, thoughts, or body sensations become useful, bringing you back into the awareness of My everlasting care, guidance, and direction.

— *G.O.D. Journals, July 2020*

INDEX CARDS

How it works may forever elude me, but in my mind there's no mystery as to why today's electronic files are stored in some elusive entity known as *the cloud*.

Considering how often I live with my head in the clouds, perpetually fearful of forgetting all I think I must remember, my better self-judgment surmises the term *cloud* likely originated from an astute observer of us atmospheric airy-fairy types.

Still, I dream. Maybe one day I will revel in what is currently beyond belief: an unshakable trust that anything I need know is always readily available, under perpetual protection, safely stored forever in some heavenly realm. Maybe then I can finally relax and have some fun.

Profession Confession: I gotta tell you, this book-writing business continues to be a fusion of profusion and confusion. I'm constantly overanalyzing every pro and con while inner combatants refuse to release their refuse. Concerned my mind contains only endless rhyme with no reason, effusion cedes conclusion: Stay amused. What else can I do?

For someone so spacy, I'm mystified as to how quickly my inner and outer storage space diminishes. Mentally and physically scattered all over the place, I carry notions about my endless notes, along with a nonstop critical narrative that regularly reminds me I have no idea how to put ideas together in a cohesive fashion. Resulting strategy: Stay busy taking everything apart while kindly (not) reassuring myself I must be making progress.

I've held a secret fantasy for decades: Upon my untimely demise, my brilliant journals and jumbled jottings will be discovered, appreciated, and assembled into a semblance of order by someone who knows how to do such things. Then I'd be honored as a posthumous genius, like Van Gogh, sans the ear-cutting part. Weird. I'm about to turn sixty-eight, and he chopped off his natural hearing aid exactly sixty-eight years before I was born. What are the chances?

One in an average of 365.25, I guess. Those damn numbers.

But as usual, I digress.

Translated: Dying is easier than attempting to do what I'm doing right (write) now.

Frustration is an invitation to clear limiting beliefs; a reminder that help is here for the asking. Trouble is, I have to first be willing to ask, but since I usually don't like the answers I receive from other humans, I rarely bother. I did, however, trust my new writing community. I had confidence they would offer fresh insight, along with a magical solution to my ongoing dilemma.

Often obsessed with doing things *the right way*, coupled with a tendency to put others *who know* on a pedestal, I decided to risk confessing the sins of my messy mind, and humbly asked for guidance on how to best organize my thoughts.

Index cards.

The intensity of my inner reaction should have been a clue: A bigger trigger was afoot.

It wasn't the first time that oft-repeated suggestion had thrown me into overwhelm, but by God, it would be the last. Just the very idea of digging for all my ideas, scattered everywhere— clouds, computers, desks, dashboards, and duffle bags of dated journals—then transferring them onto index cards, creating more unorganized clutter I wouldn't know what to do with—sent me into a deepening tale-spinning tailspin. Not happening.

With no viable solution in sight, I reattached to my familiar story problem: me. Mortification fortification spat forth. Full of hopelessness, angst, resistance, and resentment, the core belief was exposed: *I can't do anything right, and nobody can ever help me.* Sadly, my book-writing dreams would have to remain in the clouds, next to Vincent and his hairy ear.

Awareness quietly embraced the moment's Authenticity. Dejected Acceptance immediately followed, accompanied by a curious sense of clandestine, customary celebration. Ambiguously Aligned with the part of me readying to hide, seeking had ceased to be fun. My decidedly suffering stance self-righteously reaffirmed: Asking for help was useless. Innovative ideas for inspired Action were clearly nonexistent.

With nothing left to lose, relinquishment provided a subtle form of pain relief. The hell with pretty shades of pink and orange. Rising above the internal chaos, I waved the white flag.

With barely enough energy left to admit defeat, I sent a tearful, confessional email to one of my writing coaches. It was a Sunday evening, so I had no illusions about receiving an answer, and certainly not in the form it came. But surrendering aspirations of authorship left me time to do something I *did* know how to do: read.

The library's worn paperback copy of Anne Lamott's book, *Bird by Bird,* had sat, recommended but untouched, on my bedstand for weeks. Already renewed twice, it, like everything else, evoked feelings of guilt. Once again, procrastination had been keeping me from doing what I was called to do.

Jumping ahead a moment, apologies in advance for the poor quality of the photos that follow. But, please, allow me to reiterate, how very grateful I am to the part of me who heard, and heeded, whatever Guidance that prompted me to document the drama that unfolded. Left to my own devices, electronic or otherwise, this experience may have been forever lost in the clouds.

Still in the midst of breakdown, I opened the book to a random page. Here's what I saw:

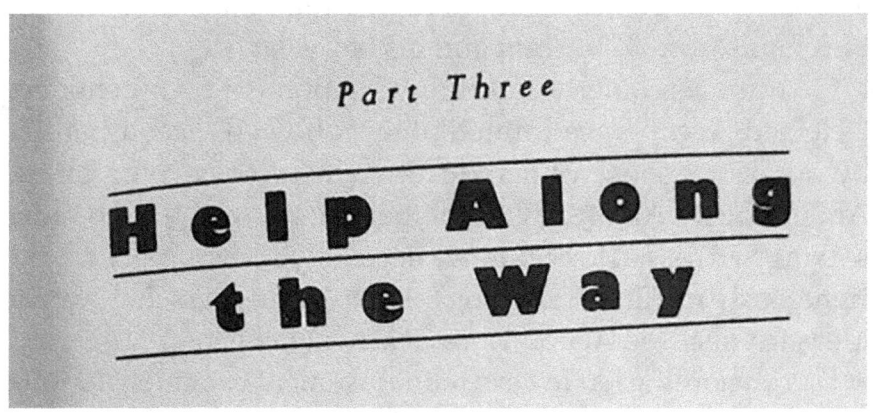

Whoa. Holy shit. Impeccable timing.
Feeling slightly encouraged; I turned the page.
No shit, I swear this is a true story.
Drum roll, please.
Here's what awaited me:

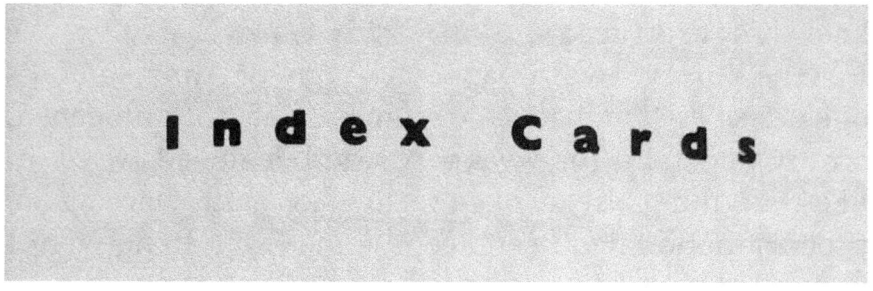

Can't make this stuff up.

On that Sunday night, of course, I had no inkling that this story would ever be shared, let alone in this it's-never-going-to-happen book you are now reading.

In case you were wondering, I still don't use index cards. The very idea still overwhelms me.

I'm learning, instead, to go with the Guidance in the moment, since even overwhelm has its messages. Unraveling the snarls that tie us to our momentary, limiting perceptions helps us recognize, and forgive, the mutiny methodology of the lower mind, clearing the way for a higher viewpoint. There will be times when undoing is more important than doing. Reversing default strategies provides energy profound with newfound courage.

Check in with the parts of yourself who tend to feel frightened, ashamed, or tempted to quit. To heal your future, you may need to grieve your past. If your current issue needs a tissue, give it what it needs, including permission to stop trying and start crying.

Your inner space adventure awaits. By accepting we aren't alone, we automatically facilitate acceptance for others. Your vulnerability invites theirs. Be true to yourself by sharing who you truly are.

Your Guidance will prompt your next action. Before, between, beyond, and back, even our most overwhelming experiences are here to show us Something always hears our current calling.

It's just lovingly waiting for your hairy inner ear to be willing to listen.

Covenant

Trusting in the Process
By surrendering to Your will
Hearing quiet voices, while
Allowing mine to still

Welcoming the fear thoughts, as
Mere lessons in illusion
To teach me transformation
And freedom from conclusion

Un-building blocks — without throwing rocks
Which keep us so apart
Allowing souls in closer
And risk opening my heart

Serving the One in front of me
By acting on Your word
Presence allows us both the gift
For Your Answer to be heard

Praising the Beloved
Honoring All as Divine
Seeing God within You
By remembering That as Mine

Channeled Poetry, May 30, 2003

CHAPTER 11

rinse and repeat

Writing from this place does not take effort; it takes your willingness to listen. As you develop the muscle and the conscious discipline of willingness, you will notice it integrating into all areas of life. Teach by being; learn by doing.

— G.O.D. Journals, March 2013

SURPRISE!

Depending on one's perspective, "Surprise!" might evoke a sense of excitement—or dread.

Seems the unexpected is always ready to party, although we aren't always ready to party with the unexpected. Those of us who are control freaks prefer to stay centered in our place of certitude, yet our only certainty is the great unknown—which tends to tango with those all-but-certain plans we oh-so-carefully planned.

I guess it's fortunate that life events are meant to be eventful. We simply can't plan for every surprise we are sure to meet along the way. Thunderstruck, wonderstruck, dazed, and amazed, the kaleidoscope of ever-shifting points of view has the capacity to be a magnificent montage of the miraculous.

Pro Tip: Plan in advance to have all future planning filled with present love. That way, anything intended as a *labor of love* doesn't just become labor. Hyperfocusing on what *might* happen keeps us from placing our focus where it's needed: *now*.

Gut-wrenching worry has a way of worming itself right into the morrow's fruition, thus spoiling tropical tidbits, available only today.

A moment of dark humor: The word *execute* was floating through my mind, initially heard in the context of intentional implementation. But perhaps you fear the time has come to pay final respects to your once-revered underground project that now appears to be dying.

It might seem like a grave situation, yet you need not succumb to passing thoughts. Even if you feel grim about what you've been reaping, you can exhume unconscious references to your heartfelt undertaking. Killjoy statements, such as: *This project is killing me*, surely weren't meant as a murderous epithet, nor destined as an epitaph. Let silliness slay you instead. Remind yourself: Your endeavor is killer.

The surprises inherent in *getting there* are certainly more enjoyable once you understand there's nowhere to get. Invite your element of surprise to join you in celebrating a co-creative journey.

You are realizing illusions of control and power are keeping you stressed and tense. In contrast, trust is what brings the joy and freedom to enjoy life's surprises. Release your plans to Me. Let your control, your addiction to outcome, become your opportunity to remember to relax and surrender. When your mind is at peace, it is available for Me to use for higher purpose.

— *G.O.D. Journals, July 2018*

Q-TIP

Ever feel a bit shocked at your reactiveness toward a noun you love or, at least at one time, remotely sort of liked? What happens to you when they don't do what you want them to do? Does upset prevail when another fails to respond to your avail? You might have noticed yourself making (perhaps accurate) assumptions that ass just doesn't give a shit about what you want.

Of course, you take it personally. But who suffers?

Our minds are quite the con artists, totally adept at drawing con-clusions. There's a part inside each of us who thinks it knows exactly how life should look. So, take some time, watch a master artist at work. Watching your mind can be quite enlightening, as you consider this soft schtick tip for the day:

Q-TIP. Quit Taking It Personally.

Nope, didn't make that one up. Wish I had.

Don't even remember where I picked it up. Have no idea as to which swabbie I should attribute.

I often notice on my walks random cotton swabs strewn about, and I take it personally. The universe, apparently, doesn't want me to forget that, no, not everything is all about me, and yes, my reactions are my responsibility. Said in another not-so-soft way, a popular slogan amongst recovery communities is: *Take the cotton out of your ears and stick it in your mouth.* Harsh.

And yes, I certainly did take that suggestion personally. After all, I have so much to say.

Getting bored with our own bullshit beliefs, ignoramus interpretations, and disempowering dialogs requires paying attention. But if there's no immediate return on our investment, we may quickly lose interest. Uprising against uprooting our upsets, we resent the space we could create in our hard little heads, simply so we would have capacity to listen a bit more closely, and maybe even learn a whole lot more.

What I am invited to notice in myself is usually spotted much more easily in another. When I'm bent on not taking a deeper dive, I can pay attention to what my fellow beings are drowning in. Unmasking the treasures in my own under-see-world can wait while I invite the outer see-world to provide valuable feedback. When I take the plunge into projection, I keep rediscovering that no one is an island, not even when marooned on It Is As It Is-Land.

Risk being real with yourself. Challenge what you think you know. Ask yourself open-ended questions that require more than a single-word answer. Try writing out those questions in longhand with your dominant hand; then let your nondominant hand answer. Its reply may surprise you; its thinking may be very different than your default inner dialog.

Consider starting with this inquiry: *What is the most powerful question I can ask you?*

Clear your inner ear, then gently listen for its heartfelt answer.

Someone inside calls for your attention.
Isn't it time you answer?

Remember, Child, the ego speaks first and loudest. Of course, it's all already been done! What I have created has always been, always will be! *I AM* not asking you to recreate the material. What *I AM* asking you to do is deliver the message to the people I send you, in your own unique way. We are in this together, you and I.

— *G.O.D. Journals, March 2012*

FIGHTING THE (NOT SO) GOOD FIGHT

Ever been taken hostage by an inanimate object?

It starts out innocently enough. The thing isn't doing what you need it to do. It stopped behaving the way it should. You're a reasonable person, so you work with it. You understand it needs time and attention. Your expertise. All you kindly ask for is its cooperation. Still, it refuses. Frustration mounts.

Suddenly, you're taking its behavior personally. Your pulse increases, your tone starts to rise. Choice cuss words escape your lips. You're busy, damn it! No time for this shit!

But pause for a second anyway. Ask the mastermind a few questions:

- Just exactly what did that object do to you? (What is it causing to happen in your world?)
- What is it making you do, feel, right now? (It did make you do it, feel it, right?)
- What value do you receive from overexpressing to something that cannot, will not, express back?

    When you've been the target of overexpression or the silent treatment, how did you react?

But maybe you're not yet willing to take a deeper look, and these annoying questions are simply serving to bring up all that anger energy you've been dying to express.

Fueled by fury, you go back to focusing on the object of your upset. *Maybe if I kick it, hit it, or swear at it, it will cooperate. Screw that. I'm going to kill it!*

Rational, right?

And there, your projected noun quietly sits, totally unreactive to your reactions. Calmly staring you down, it has the audacity to revel in its smug observation of your behavior. By default, it wins. Again.

When it seems you can't hear, it's simply because the voice that doesn't want to hear has taken over. There is a part of your mind that is always at choice. No matter what the situation, when you access the chooser, an awareness of opportunity for momentary decision, you are in a state of empowerment.

— *G.O.D. Journals, September 2014*

Still, ego hates losing. In moments of insanity, convinced it still holds the power, it makes one last desperate controlling attempt. *I'll show you, you freakin' piece of garbage! Into the landfill you go!* The brilliant ego has allowed an emotionless, thoughtless object to control your emotions, thoughts, and behavior.

Unplugged from Source, we may unconsciously try to get power from nouns, outcomes, and fixes that have no power to give us anything. Having seemingly lost our Mind, we become momentary victims of our own artificial intelligence. In our attempts to rule a kingdom of objects, is it any wonder they react in revolting, objectional ways?

Energetic flow has a way of making its presence known, inviting emotion to be what it is: energy in motion. Maybe the object's momentary revolution is actually objective, somehow knowing exactly what we need to make room for our revelation. Amped up? Feeling charged? Ungrounded? Shocked? Zapped? Clingy? Discover what's beyond static.

Rapscallion or angel, our reactions merely provide feedback, simply pointing to the current empowered mindset. Staying plugged in to the nonsense in our noggins will, eventually, cause overload, resulting in caustic battery leakage. When whatever utilities you've been utilizing are just putting off the inevitable decision to get current with your power source, it's time to ground yourself in a safe alternative.

Be willing to discover the causal, controlling mechanisms underneath your power struggles with soul-er energy. The Source of your being has infinite ways to energize you, providing you are willing to plug into that which you prefer to receive.

Welcome the lessons, the learning. Watch and observe yourself, as you would a playful child. Be awake within the dream. Let creation be yours. Embrace to enlighten.

— *G.O.D. Journals, September 2014*

Have you ever noticed that inanimate objects seem more prone to rebellion when your energy is overwhelmingly overloaded? What an opportune time to surrender your upset and consciously shift potential meltdown into a more conducive energy!

Experimenting with this stuff can be electrifying. Noticing my own fried mindset is the sign that I must first unplug, then plug back into a working outlet, and recharge. More often than not, transferring my transformation to said inanimate object by silently sending it a little love, light, and appreciation either miraculously resets the object, or allows me to receive clear Guidance as to the next steps. Ah, transformers.

Rather than use broken behaviors you know will upset you, experiment with new possibilities. Give your attention to your intention. Look through the lens of lightness. Every moment is here to contribute to your enlightenment.

You can always change your mind, and therefore your actions. And your outcome.

Ask Me to clear the judgments as soon as you notice them. Your connection is dependent on conscious connection to Me. Stay in action, without judging the preparation work or the perceived outcome. Allow Guidance. Trust it. Stop comparing yourself to others. Instead, My Love, trust your flow. Tune in to your experience, your authenticity.

— *G.O.D. Journals, June 2012*

STOP FEARING THE CLEARING

When your heart is no longer all aflutter catching sight of that clutter, those outworn items might be starting to wear on you.

Having once shared a meaningful relationship, particular segments of your physical, mental, or emotional memorabilia might be peskily pestering for some loving attention. With a vague sense something other than dust has been collecting on your collectibles, you might become busy, forgetful, or willfully neglectful, preferring not to admit that your previously treasured treasures no longer hold the same magic.

Next, you might retreat into the eternal stage of *getting ready*. Letting go of the olden days can feel like a loss of identity, so deferment might seem like a somewhat safe place to park yourself as you ponder the distinct possibility you may never be fully ready to recover from, nor release, that charm you once cherished. Having no idea how to come to terms with what somehow needs to be done—let alone how to go about doing it—it may seem easier to just shelve, right along with them, their plea for honor. And incompletion looms.

When moments of bemusement arise, finding amusement in the English language is clearly my favored distractor. Dillydallying on dealing with dilemmas concerning collectibles, this word-collector recollects the word *dust*.

As a noun, *dust* is a pesky, losing battle.

As a verb, *dust* implies lovingly caring for said collectibles.

Clinging to the hope that incompletions will stay in the background, continually blowing themselves off, probably collects more remorse and, eventually, more work. The longer we avoid dealing with that-bric-a-brac-that-needs-to-be-dealt-with, the bigger the project—and guilty projections—can seem.

It's helpful to distinguish between the various meanings we've attached to our preoccupations. People, patterns, paraphernalia; perhaps it's the thoughts and emotions we've collected around them that keep us from dealing with them. So for a moment, let whatever it is be what it is—a neutral noun—while compassionately acknowledging your associated stories.

Awareness that unfinished business is imminent doesn't make the unfinished business immediate. Re-mind yourself: You really don't want to end up resenting someone, or something, you once revered. You know where to take it from here.

Authenticity doesn't want you to miss today by pretending you live in the past or the future. *Acceptance* trusts whatever thoughts or emotions are present, while quietly questioning your current state of *alignment*. Kindly *ask* yourself what one next *action* could be. No commitments necessary. You're just exploring options, while conveniently dusting off your Straight-A Strategy.

Completion is a process, not an event. Honor those once-cherished memories that ask for your attention. Touch them in some manner—mentally, physically, emotionally. You can always put them back on the shelf. You need no longer judge yourself for any unconscious guilt for not dealing with what, eventually, you think you must.

Because, in a way—your way—you really just did.

Let precious moments of awareness add to your treasure trove of mementos. This counts as one of those times you consciously practiced loving self-care.

I AM guiding you. Change is always in process. You are developing your awareness, and together, we are building a foundation. Right now, you are attached to external forms. It is your attachment that keeps you in judgment of the process. Notice the mirrors of attraction. They are a result of what you chose to do, who you chose to be, in the preceding now.

— *G.O.D. Journals, May 2012*

WISHY-WASHY

Speaking of mirrors, does one's proclivity toward tolerating chronically smudged screens, windows, and glasses reflect one's lack of clarity? My fingerprints, everywhere. I have to take responsibility. That habit of deciding, in advance, certain chores will be unpleasant only encourages innovative evasion strategies.

Whether or not my inner groundhog recognizes its shadow, luring that goading little badger out of its burrow is half the battle. Thriving on tasty tidbits of guilt, it launches its brilliant counterattack utilizing compulsive overload. From laziness to craziness, it knows if it tears everything apart with its sharp incisors, a bigger mess will be created. Intuitively sensing I won't be able to stand it for long, its gnawing logic is to punish, from *doing nothing* to forcing me to deal with that-which-I-wish-I-had-never-started.

How many more times must I suffer through this cycle? Where does all this useless self-torture energy go? Might it really all come out in the wash? Whoa, just found a couple of crumpled pink flags carelessly tossed in the hamper. Where did those come from? Heavy load. Heavier sigh.

I know, I saw you sigh. But that was good—because you took a breath! You noticed your mind wandering, closed your eyes, waited for insight. Now here you are, back listening and writing. See how good it feels just to stretch? It really helps to move the energy around.

— *G.O.D. Journals, December 2011*

Hey, at least airing my dirty laundry helps keep me from being so clothes-minded.

I'm grateful I've spent the last half-century or so integrating this insight: When the pain of *not* doing something becomes greater than the preconceived pain I've associated with doing it, I'll finally just do it. But it's sort of heartbreaking, realizing I'm making myself endure more pain, guilt, and shame while waiting to trick myself into action.

If you have a tendency for extremes concerning your daily practices (totally wishy-washy or compulsively awash) you might experience chronic agitation. Those stubborn stains on our characters often require pre-treatment, along with endless rinsing and repeating. But perhaps we're just one detergent pod short of immaculacy. So, stop hanging yourself out to dry.

Dirty laundry is just another opportunity to start a new cycle.

Rushing around, getting stuff done so you have time to connect later is missing the point. The only thing you are ever really avoiding is Me. Stop the cycle. Do it differently. What is the payoff in being disconnected, other than a feeble attempt to strengthen your ego? And what would be the purpose of that? Stay by My side, Dear One; all you need is right here.

— *G.O.D. Journals, January 2012*

STOP CRYING TOWEL PLAY

Dash into action! We'll end this chapter by seeing how many deterrent wordplays we can find while softening the fabric of our being. Dreamily Dreft into your story. See how it All weaves together? Imagine how Fab it would be if we'd be Bold enough to stop taking life so Persil-y. Cheer up! Surf turns with every Tide. You'll never Gain anything by beating yourself with an Arm and Hammer.

If your cycle of feeling drained keeps spinning you out of control, it only means you took on too heavy of a load. Rebalance. Next time, opt for the gentle cycle. Accept the reality that things will sometimes fall apart before you even notice they need mending. To stretch, handle your material in a new way. Wherever you are in your cycle, now is always a great time to lovingly create your future. Stop clinging to the familiar. Have fun watching life's little wrinkles smooth themselves out.

Oh, the irony. Oh, the ironing. Rinse and repeat.

Break the cycles that keep you asleep to your Spirit, so you become increasingly aware that all the Guidance you ever need is already here. That is what you were brought here to learn, to teach, to be.

— *G.O.D. Journals, February 2012*

CHAPTER 12

crack yourself up and open

Clearing whatever judgments, fears, or ego-thoughts that are in the way is paramount to receiving Direction. Notice the blocks being reflected both inside and out, as both giver and receiver. What must you move out of the way, or put in place, so the flow is directed, and keeps moving, with steady purpose and clear intention?

— *G.O.D. Journals, March 2012*

REFLECTING

To expend life's precious moments aligning with something that isn't aligned is to wrestle with illusions. What do we get from getting in our own way? Intrusive or instructive, my inner world's cast of characters, each with their own special knack to distract, all claim their expertise lies in offering unsolicited, insistent, and inconsistent advice, erroneous time management tips in particular.

Admittedly, my curiosity was recently piqued when I heard Ms. Guided suggest I take another break and play with the word *reflection*. Serving as a deflection, she encouraged me to turn away from the harsh voice of Ms. Judgment, who was loudly urging me to reflect upon what I was (not) accomplishing.

Turns out, the root meaning of *flect* is "bend."

Perhaps every oblique obfuscation is meant as exercise (*flect*, two-three-four; *flect*, two-three-four!) in order to integrate flexibility. Practice going with the flow. Bend into becoming. Lean into learning. Uplift the mindset.

Navigating through our darker rabbit holes must, by definition, be a hole-y adventure. Clarity will surely dawn upon us, post-emergence, in the light of day. When we no longer fear giving in (to who knows whom), giving up (to who knows what), or going in (to who knows where), demanding dispositions simply become another wakeup call.

The value of time reflects profundity in present moment awareness. You can't do life wrong, so bend with today's teachings. Besides, brawling with beguilements is bootless.

Ironic that the word *rest* is embedded in *wrestle*. Time for a nap.

You must be willing to see your personal illusions to let them go. You cannot hold onto hurt, fear, resentment, or worry and expect to experience or demonstrate peace of mind. Child, stay with Me. Bear witness to those I send to you. Monitor your resistance and surrender it to Me.

— *G.O.D. Journals, May 2019*

FOLLOWING CLUES

Playing junior detective has long been my idea of fun.

As a tween, my go-to escapes included daydreaming, overeating, and obsessively reading Nancy Drew mystery stories, becoming rather adept at doing all three at once. Kindhearted Nancy had an intuitive knack for uncovering random ways to be of assistance while remaining poised, confident, and steadfast under stress. Dependable, discerning, and determined, Nancy's deductive reasoning and leadership qualities were admirably intertwined with wisdom, patience, and faith.

Putting Nancy on the perfection pedestal was probably my first mistake. Certain that good fortune must be the driving force of fortitude, my undercover story was drenched in secret resentment. My dreamy self never dreamed that Nancy, nor anyone else, ever suffered from doubts or insecurities like I did. It was easier to treasure the belief that I, alone, was alone. No one I knew spoke of anything *real*—so my quest to become unreal had to become very real.

In short, I became a brilliant critical thinker. Very critical.

Taking on a pretentious role called forward my great pretender, all too happy to support me in looking for and finding, mind you, evidential evidence about others' flaws. Overlooking the fact that my fabrications were a quilt of questionable bits and pieces, designed to cover my own insecurities, I found it comforting to continue concluding my conclusions must be correct.

Holding a magnifying glass to things outside oneself is a handy way to avoid the mirrors and messages inside. But mysteriously, life's wisdom manages to keep weaving the most annoying characteristics of others into our awareness while leaving our own looming projects tied up in knots.

You have always been attracted to metaphor, meaning, and mystery, expressing a desire to live life guided by Spirit. What if there were no mystery about it? What if it was only your ego that makes things seem so intricate, complicated, convoluted, hidden? Simplify, my Child. Have fun with that childlike joy of yours, that enthusiasm.

— *G.O.D. Journals, June 2012*

Viscerally vexed with the trendy term *life coach*, my annoyed armchair assessor persisted in insisting the label was both over-used and under-scrutinized. Initiating an invitation to play *Let's Make a Deal* with the gentler aspects of my critically acclaimed inner co-conspirators, we resolved our special case by just making a damn decision: Let go of whoever the hell you are trying to be —and just be who you are. Today I affectionately alternate between referring to myself as a Divine Demonstrator, a Spiritual Life Coach, a Reflective Detective, an Authenticity Advocate, and a Truth Sleuth. Take your pick.

You, too, are called. Devote yourself to sleuthing for your truth. Allow each discovery to play a role in being your guide. Normalize nonstarters while you wander and wonder. You're bound to encounter foreboding and remorse along the way, not to mention a nearly intolerable temptation to turn back toward the familiar. So what? You're getting a clue, so find out what it needs from you. Then, keep going.

Releasing habitual interpretations, every clue reveals its own value, in its own time. Expect to uncover unexpected treasure. Learn to discern what needs closer examination, and what can be set aside for now.

Every "no shit, Sherlock" moment is a precursor for you to "know shift, Sherlock."

You are wondering if this journey is not so much bringing more love and light into the world, but rather uncovering it. What if it is already there, and your job is to discover it? Are you willing to take on the treasure hunt today?

— *G.O.D. Journals, June 2013*

RE-COGNIZING COGNITION

Thanks, internet, for the re-minder. Reflective Detective has just rediscovered that *cognize* is a verb.

For some of us, getting into action is half the battle—perhaps a moment for us to re-cognize the possibility we might be in resistance. So, let's shred the trench coat and get into the trenches.

Authenticity Advocate is all about finding new, renowned ways to re-know oneself, while Truth Sleuth regularly reminds the lower mind it would actually prefer to show up in its empowered truth.

The power to change one's mindset, to upend and transcend upset, is always an inside job. Utilizing a moment of re-flection, we exercise new posse-abilities. With proper support, we can build our strength as we practice bending with what is, exactly where we are and no matter who we are with. Staying stiff, stuck, and oh-so-set in our stagnant stories gets painful after a while.

Re-flection is a pre-cursor (sure, go ahead, swear first if need be) to re-cognition, re-minding us that re-set is actually a viable option. Familiar re-activity calls for action, including deactivation of thoughts of inaction. No matter what you're in the midst of, you're still in the midst.

Frightened illusions are merely prospects for apparition alteration. When situations seem out of alignment with essence, uncover what is hiding. Forgiving ghosts of the past keeps them from stealing your currency. In the light of your presence, energy vampires are nonexistent. Lessons re-presented (you know, regifting the present) need not be haunting, daunting, or leaving you wanting. Stop ghosting yourself. Employ the ethers.

Pro Tip: Play specter-detector! Scheme with your stealthier sides.

That which is scaring you is dying to share with you. Fear not, frightened self. Since "the shadow knows," (heh-heh-heh) hear its perspective. It's been demanding your attention, to woo-woo you into recognizing the futility of hanging out with the inner critic and other shady characters. Phantom selves, re-cognized, disappear, so the next clue can appear. Woo them out of the shadows of your mind. Decode their messages. Spy on them, through the peerless, self-corrective binoculars of self-forgiveness; releasing any peer projections, thus improving your overall outlook.

When the invisible no longer has any ability to frighten us, we'll recapture the disappearing energy we unconsciously expended on being someone we weren't—and reinvest it in who we are.

The current opportunity is to re-member your membership in the One Mind, to re-cognize (become aware, again and again) that *I AM* always here to guide you in your purpose in this moment. That is all you ultimately need to know—or want.

—*G.O.D. Journals, January 2016*

218

TREAT YO'SELF WITH CON-FUSION

Antipathy antithesis: Treat yourself to a lifepath you love.

If you are prone to retreat amongst habits or personas meant to keep your suffering secure, stay aware of any probation vibration. A little extra hibernation, a new form of libation. Excess treats will trick us right back into oblivious overindulgence.

Since misery does love company, notice any miserable company you've been keeping—in body, mind, or spirit. If you are growing weary of cohorts who conspire to co-sign your misery, re-cognize this may be a re-minder of a renowned form of commiseration. Seeing others or ourselves as fractured might be a sneaky way to take a break from facing that which we fear is broken within. Breakdown, like Mary's little lamb, is sure to follow.

But reaching your breaking point might be your best break yet.

When ensnared in enmeshment, it's common to have booming thoughts drumming in. Remember that familiar call to beat the doldrums? Once again, it's just encouraging energy release. Whatever we do, wherever we go, may seem like moments of critical choice. Ironically, though, choosing criticism never helps. Self-compassion is the compass that re-turns us toward inspired intentionality.

Granted, entwining oneself in the interim can be uncomfortable. But be comforted in knowing discomfort need not last. Re-treat yourself with reality: You just aren't privy to all that is forever unfolding. The key is to accept everything as your transitory guide, right back into your next certain steps into certain uncertainty.

Pure thoughts coming from Source are focused on loving intention. They energize and add to the sum total of conscious awareness. Confusion is not necessary, but it is habitual. Awareness of your thoughts will help diffuse any misperceptions.

— *G.O.D. Journals, September 2014*

So, let's play with breaking down confusing breakdowns by breaking down confusion, shall we? Con. Fusion.

Con: Synonymous with fraud, deception, swindle. As a prefix: with, together. Ego's fragile fraudulence is counter to having its contradictions called out, conning us into controlling and conflicting conduct. Then, confoundingly, we contest calling upon contemplative consultants, leaving us to conclude, somewhat accurately, we must be out of our minds. Neglecting to fuse with Higher Mind is bound to confuse us. That's okay, we'll always get another chance.

Fuse: Conveniently, fuse can be confusing. Is *fuse* ready to merge or rage? Is it connected or charged? Whatever your refuse, refusing to acknowledge it will likely re-fuse any short fuse that's seriously ready to blow. Active energy causes re-actions. *Dynamite!* Plugging right along, it might be time to retreat from any con who energetically keeps you from fusing with your True Self. Remember, you cannot be unplugged from Source. Even when you can't seem to stay powered up for long, the light of your Guidance still waits in your shadow, oblivious to whatever confusing story you're currently plugged into.

Your Soul-er Power source is available. Use it.

You are hearing this Voice, again, because of your willingness to listen, tune in. A moment ago, your thought about confusion made sense—taking the word con + fusion and thinking of it as fused with. Duality is confusing—two forces working against one another. You are currently fused with, attached to, many voices.

— *G.O.D. Journals, January 2012*

REAL-IZING REALITY

Who in you does the real-izing? That is, who in you decides what's real, worthy of your attention?

I'll wager we've all granted unconscious dominion to the most unrealistic parts of ourselves; that is, whoever inside we've identified with in the moment. Often, that's probably been the loudest, most fearful, or most self-righteous parts of the persona—in other words, whoever we momentarily re-cognized as *us*.

For the sake of argument—there's nothing like a good inner fight to ramp up awareness—become cognizant in recognizing that to which you commonly kowtow: the persons, places, practices, or processes that most predictably provoke your most caustic reactions.

Blaming *x* for causing your distress makes sense. After all, if *x* hadn't *x*-ed, you wouldn't be perturbed or disturbed. You've been wronged; *self-righteousness is right!* With perfect acclaim, *claim victory!*

Empowering, right? Strong emotions can be surprisingly energizing in the moment.

Except moments morph. Awareness kicks back in. Pondering the *x* situation, you real-ize a predominance of annoyance. *X* is still dominating, front and center, yet is nowhere to be seen. So from where does this irritation originate? *Not fair!* lower mind grumbles. X *caused this! I have every right to stay upset!*

Of course you do! But why would you?

Real-ization dawns again. What benefits are you receiving from staying upset? If the price isn't worth the penalty, it's time to break free. Your sign to re-mind, re-align is nigh. Fortunately, you can also real-ize the fact that infinite responsibility need only be taken one instant at a time.

Real-izing who holds the key to your prison grants you the freedom you seek.

Relax into Higher Guidance. It's always here, but it's up to you to actually follow it. You must bring your illusions to Me in order for Me to transmute them. Choose carefully, Child. Which thoughts will you hold onto today? It is a gift to Me when you freely give Me what doesn't serve, so you experience the inner freedom you so desire.

— *G.O.D. Journals, May 2015*

Since we're always dealing with ideas and ideals, inane and insane, why not decide to real-ize every experience is here in service, meant to contribute to our collective joy? As a matter of fact, momentary interpretations have never been a matter of fact, but a matter of choice.

Some version of inner diversion always magically appears at the appointed time—watching the mind playing with pondering. Might *alize* (as in re-*alize*) hold yet another message?

Ignore the judge; follow the nudge.

Well, well, well, Google has apparently re-alized that Alize is a feminine name, of Hebrew origin.

It means "joyful."

Stay with Me, Child. I have never left you. Your fears of the future are based on illusion, perception. Fear keeps you from experiencing Me in the present. Sink back into your awareness of Me. When you realize, once again, that you are enveloped in love, and always have been, fear simply dissolves, becomes nonexistent.

— *G.O.D. Journals, June 2020*

RE: SENT, TIRE, LEASE, TURN

Sometimes, we just gotta to go there to real-ize we don't gotta go there anymore.

Déjà vu. Where and why have you been sent, then re-sent, right back into re-sent-ment?

Retiring in a state of resentment might resonate with those who experience a sense of safety living amongst the naysayers. Rarely required to re-tire their re-treading stories, they prefer to drive their resentments home, rather than enjoying the ride of their lives. Tiring.

Stop. Look. Listen.

Drive down a new avenue. Pick a venue. Always time for a little play, at least on words.

If the lion's share of the rental space in your mind is regularly leased to lyin' tigers, potential precariousness prevails. The preciousness of your inner real-ty becomes your reality. Sure, noisy inner neighbors are a nuisance, but they're there to awaken you, to help you real-ize your field of dreams has become a nightmare. Imagine living re-sent-ment-free. Awareness of where you frequently find yourself, or perhaps more poignantly, lose yourself, is valuable real estate.

Find the part of your Mind that already knows. Aware of ongoing inner conversations, your job is to quiet the other mind long enough to tune in. This takes two things: willingness and practice. Child, stay with Me. Monitor your personal illusions and resistance. Surrender them to Me. Teach transformation through demonstration.

— *G.O.D. Journals, May 2019*

The place in your mind where inner peace resides continually calls. Your perpetual invitation to re-turn toward your Sender is nigh. The messages you send, blindly or carbon copied, are continually forwarded to addresses unknown, so be sure whatever you're sending out is in alignment with what you wish to receive.

A friend just shared on one of my social media accounts their excitement about the pending release of this book. The way it was typed, the word *release* showed up as *real ease*. Fully cognizant of the part of my mind tempted to obsesses about something I'm not yet ready to do—let alone having any idea how to do it, plus zero control over outcome—my G.O.D. found a way to send a re-minder, with real ease. Message received.

Granted, any shift into a new mental neighborhood is challenging. You have no idea who or what you'll find there. But once you stop questioning the courageous moves that must be made, there's peaceful re-sign-ation. Re-lease requires re-signing a new lease on life, a graceful lead to a new frontier. If you've been living in the land of the lost, re-list with a divine real-tor; one who works soul-y on co-mission, whose sole mission is to share in collective re-mission.

Higher Mind never requires a piece of land; it only requires inner peace to land.

Your divine plot and purpose await.

Who in you still thinks you must do this journey alone? Who in you reminded you to listen for this Direction? Despite distraction, it's always here, and you still hear. Hasn't this been the case all along? Stay the Course. Your willingness integrates your understanding at deeper levels. Being sure of our connection requires connecting. You are being shown; for as you learn, so will you teach.

— *G.O.D. Journals, April 2020*

CRACK YOURSELF UP

What if your yoke really was easy, and your burden light?

The egghead in me has always had a sunny upside, loving any good yolk-yolk that would crack me up.

Connecting to yourself in ways that feel safely aligned with your authenticity is probably the best way to get to know your inner Guidance. *Paronomasia* (the plague of the punster) has proven itself to be one of my most reliable go-to-protectors. It even found ways to team up with my frightened-of-spirituality-alphabet-soup-stoner-self back in the 1970s.

At the time, the book and movie, *The Exorcist* was frighteningly popular. Noting the backward spellings of *evil* and *devil* brought some comfort, yet persistent fiendish fears required me to constantly look for creative ways to leave those burning, unanswerable questions on the back burner. As I became playful with the petrifying, punning preempted my paranoiac pondering concerning an apparent predestination to burn in hell for all eternity.

Aptly calling it *The Eggsorcist*, I fantasized about opening a futuristic egg-themed café. Specialty dish: deviled eggs. Restroom signs would read HENS and COCKS.

The fear of the unknown keeps us sitting on the fence of defense. Trying not to face what's in our face, once we've stayed five seconds too long, our teeter becomes totter. Picket or pitchfork, whatever's poking at our posterior, hear discomfort's discomfiting message: *Leap or fall, Humpty-Dumpty!*

Have some compassion for whatever's egging you on. Life's hard-boiled experiences would leave anyone fried. Feeling poached, we've scrambled to survive. Not all the king's horses, nor all the king's men, could put Humpty together again; so as the saying goes, let your cracks be where your light comes in.

It's time to courageously eggs-press yourself. Get eggs-cited about all you are here to bring. Let the cracks in your shell signify new emergence, showing that you know you will be shown new, co-creative ways to put yourself together again.

This is not a fix. This is a remembering. Treat yourself and others with compassion as you learn. Has your experience not been showing you when you quiet your mind and ego's agenda while releasing any attempt to fix what is not broken, here *I AM*, in the midst?

— *G.O.D. Journals, February 2012*

NEW-YOU RE-SOLUTIONS

Messes can't mess with us when we allow ourselves to be where we are.

Go ahead, fall apart. Anything but peaceful, scatter yourself, piecemeal. Strewn energy rearranges your view so you can re-view — from an elevated perspective. All apart, yet still all a part of, there's a bigger picture we can't yet see.

When I typed the words *my stories*, the word *mysteries* mysteriously appeared. Mind vacillating. Puzzled. Familiar dilemma. Can one trust in life's ability to re-solve itself? An issue I thought was resolved is now re-presenting itself as unsolvable. Heavy sigh. Whoa, just saw *unsolvable* as *unlovable*. Is this moment revealing the juxtaposition of a subconscious position?

We each bring our individuality, our piece of the divine puzzle, to a grand picture, blessedly designed to eternally reveal itself. You might be tempted to see your part as insignificant. But it's the tiny pieces that offer the clues to discover what's missing.

Answer to My Prayer

I feel so sad and lonely
Like I'm ten years old again
A heart wrenching feeling
That I never have fit in

My soul seems so divided
Both want to play and judge
Can't decide which way to go
So I'll stay here and begrudge

Somehow feel so different
Don't know how to just join in
Or if I even want to—seems
I'm on the outside looking in

Desperately focused on circumstance
Again I know I've lied
One lesson life has taught me
From my Self I cannot hide

Now I'm stuck and angry
What scapegoat can I blame
'Cause if I risk going in
I'll feel that deeper pain

Yet the soul within keeps pleading
Please give these thoughts a voice
Stop living fibs and say what is
No longer have a choice

So I went within and asked Him
Just how to work this through
Now willing to see it differently
And get His point of view

Suddenly it occurred to me
It can't be alone I am
And if we'd each just tell our truth
We'd dissolve this cryptogram

The result was this story
That with you now I've shared
And if authenticity has helped you heal,
It was an answer to my prayer.

Channeled Poetry, January 2003

Puzzling problems tend to exhaust us before they exhaust themselves. Yet every piece will, eventually, fit. Start by looking for edgy alignment, bringing awareness and authenticity to the staging area. Accepting what is so, we can discern which pieces of today's puzzle-rama-o-drama are ours to find.

Play with the idea that *cure* is rooted in *obscure*. Innovative information precedes transformation. Maybe not having it all together is the adventure of a lifetime; perhaps personal unraveling is meant to untangle that ubiquitous re-minder: In our asking for direction, we are asked to listen for an answer.

The New You Re-Solution is re-solved by staying awake to the fact that we don't have the power to put all the pieces together before their time. But waiting is much more enjoyable when we're listening to Father Time, here to re-mind us our present moment is our most renewable gift. No need to wait for special holidays. Every day is a holy day.

Resolve to keep re-solving. When your mind just can't wrap itself around what's happening, wrap yourself around the present instead. A New-You re-solution will continually present itself. Open the gift of now. The gifts you bring were probably precognitively pre-sent, but it's likely your readiness to receive — and be — the gift you are is a pre-recognition requirement.

Forgiveness is for-giving. Give Me any thought that disturbs you. Give Me your judgments, your worries, your upsets; there is no reason for you to shoulder the burden. Instead, let Me show you the power of a changed mind. Surrender. Let go of control. Give it all to Me, so you experience transformation.

— *G.O.D. Journals, September 2015*

RE-SOURCE-FULL

The Source of all Creation may not be predictable, but it's certainly reliable.

Life keeps unfolding, and creation keeps creating. Source remembers for you what you thought you forgot: Your very nature is renewable energy, forever full of the Source that created it. Your unique contribution is essential to your environment.

Transcend procrastination by becoming an active partner in co-creation. Humbly ask to be re-Sourced, refilled with natural, divine re-creation. But recreational activities require you to join in the fun, so stop taking yourself so damn seriously. Enlighten up. Experiment.

And heed fair warning: Integration sometimes requires wading through the swamps of interrogation, where those inner in-terror-gators hide. We get over dark and murky fears by mindfully walking through them.

We know what bears do in those peat-mossy woods. Still, good advice bears witness and bears repeating: Re-peat (re-fertilize) as necessary. That's what this shit is for.

Mystery solved.

Reflections

Trying to find you, while
Crying to find me
This is what they said was love
Must tread so carefully

Terrified by you, then
Verified by me
How can I unlock my heart
Can't even find the key

Scared of losing you, worse
I might lose me
If we're both love's prisoner
How can we be free

Feeling safe with you, now
Receive this love from me
Reflections for each other's light
Through the dark we'll see

Presence found in you, finds
Presence now in me
As we enter two-by-two
We join in unity

God in you I see
Reflected back in me
Open to the truth we find
We're One so naturally

Channeled Poetry, July 2002

232

CHAPTER 13

embracing your ex

None of this has to go in the book. You are excited
about a new level, a surge of willingness to actively
bring your learnings to others. But remember,
ego thrives on extremes. Excessive work, then
procrastination. Getting lost in trying to figure things
out, in advance. Those strategies only serve to cover
up your conscious connection with Me. The truth is,
of course, you are always connected. Remember to
listen for the Still Small Voice of Love.

— *G.O.D. Journals, September 2018*

Expect the unexpected.

With the intention to expedite an expedition into finding
the perfect G.O.D. message with which to open this chapter,
I put only *ex* into the search bar of my messages folder. The
above message, from seven years ago, appeared; referencing not

only several *ex* words, but a concept called "the book" —barely extant in the ethers, and certainly nonexistent in the physical.

Exchanging exasperations for the exceptional and profound continues to be the crux of my journey. The essence of my inner explorer yearns for expansion, knowing all of life as extraordinary. Imagine the exponential possibilities as the awareness of love's omnipresence becomes an exciting excursion amongst all fellow travelers.

Still, defenses exacerbate. Ego's importance insists on exaggerating itself. Addicted to extremism, it dramatically sees itself nowhere betwixt extraordinary and extra-ordinary. Every experience must be exceptional, insuring it can stay wrapped in its victim stance of exclusion. In the ego's exhausting determination to dominate, it must prove itself to be the exception to every rule; thus, assuring its own excommunication.

After all, the ego doesn't want us to communicate from our higher selves. That would require it to surrender drama and control. *Extra, extra, read all about it!* Calling ourselves out on an exceptional story extravaganza requires exhaling and bringing awareness to our collective craving for excitement designed to mask our fears.

But of what are we so afraid?

Consider all the exes you'd prefer to just expel, ex off your list, send into exile, pretending they never existed. The extra exertion it will take to get to a place of exoneration within yourself is exactly why you've excused yourself from dealing with them in the first place. But look at it this way: Whatever's been exaggerated in your exigent life experience is designed to support you in a whole new level of excellence.

Lessons that exhibit exaction contain offers to examine feedback. Although extracting your earlier exam results does require further study and homework, don't excoriate yourself for any perceived ex-ante failures. Everyone has experienced forgetting our most basic life lesson.

Fortunately, that course in self-forgiveness happens to be perpetual.

Tune in to awareness that constant Love and Guidance are already yours to embrace, embody, share, and teach. Forgetting only leads to deeper commitment, re-learning, and practice. Be gentle with your process. There is no arrival, for you are already here. Expand your mind evermore, that it may include whatever you've previously rejected through projection. Embrace and expand your inner peace to erase and disband your illusions.

— *G.O.D. Journals, July 2013*

EXES TO EXCEPT

Where, what, when, with whom, and under which circumstances do you make exceptions? Who is the someone or something you just can't or won't forgive? What parts of the story remain incomplete?

- *Exhibit A:* Excessively exclaiming you are so exceedingly over them/it, yet exorbitant complaints and attachment to surrounding drama continually demand your poor exhausted audience to support your saga. Awareness and authenticity check.

- *Exhibit B:* Seeing the exceptions you've made might exacerbate an exasperating experience if you allow it to do so. Don't. Instead, accept. Forgive yourself for not seeing and doing what you weren't yet ready to see or do.

- *Exhibit C:* Extensive expression is a clue. You know it's time to exit the expressway to completion. But since x still seems to be in your way, consider: What's out of alignment? Who keeps changing lanes, preventing x from exiting?

- *Exhibit D:* Having asked for trusted input, a time may come when you decide it's inappropriate for someone or something to continue to exist in your periphery, necessitating extraction. When there's excommunication, it may no longer be suitable to communicate with an ex. Things fall apart. They reach their expiration date. Check in with your expertise, as it's expected you'll want to avoid stepping into excrement.

- *Exhibit E:* Everyone has experienced relationships, life situations, inanimate objects, thought patterns, emotions, and so on, that worked then, but don't work now. There was a time when your shared experience served. Your action today, from the sanctity and safety of Higher Mind, holds the knowing there's no need to expel loving memories.

There's no excuse to harbor feelings of victimization, resentment, or anger. Lift your anchor; expedite an expedition into new exploratory territory. Take a leisurely cruise. See where your flow takes you. Embarking on an inner excursion is a journey into embracing your excellency. Your unfolding life is truly one of exaltation, since no one else will ever have your exact experience. Make the most of it.

Exemplify your exquisite story, then step beyond it.

Be aware (beware!) of the stories you are holding onto—for dear life—as you now know it. Whom or what have you not completely forgiven? Re-experience those experiences so you can literally work them out of you. When you finally surrender them to Me, fully and completely, you will find inner peace is already yours. It is here, with Me, waiting for you, in the heart of forgiveness.

— *G.O.D. Journals, December 2015*

EMBRACING YOUR EX-TENSION

Remember, life is our classroom.

And some lessons can be pretty tough. Luckily, though, experiential extension courses are universally available. Once we're ready to separate from the stressful tales we've tired of telling, our present tension can finally become our ex-tension.

But this is adult education. You may first be required to:

- Neutrally notice how much tension your thoughts about *x* have caused you.
- Compassionately embrace experiences as growth opportunities.
- Allow yourself to learn from the Head Heart Director of Extension Courses.

You'll also be expected to explore extensive new possibilities, co-creating exercises that work for you. For example, you might start by executing an exaltation agreement between you and yourself while considering what might have to happen for an experience you've been shrouding in anger, fear, or guilt to extend into an expression of love and forgiveness.

Don't worry. You needn't examine curricula all at once. There probably isn't anything that needs immediate exorcism, expulsion, or excavation. But invite your awareness to be honest. When, where, and with whom do you typically exhibit excellence or extraordinary challenge? Allow curiosity to reveal exulted patterns. Embrace what is so. Extravaganza! Exploring for the sake of expansion is exciting.

Join in partnership, extending compassionate inclusion to all parts of yourself. Exchange your default-self for your no-fault self. Every moment is merely an excerpt, so serves as an example.

Extra credit: Expand that no-fault mindset to an outer ex; for example, a wasband or past-wife experience.

After all, what is truly true for one must be truly true for all. No exceptions.

The Christ Mind is continuous clarity. Clearing comes from being willing to release that which no longer serves. Changes are challenging because of your human attachment to thoughts, things, objects, and outcomes. Attachments become burdensome after a period of trial and error. Love is never a burden, for its extension frees you to feel My Presence.

— *G.O.D. Journals, June 2020*

EMBRACING EXCUSES AND EXPECTATIONS

Explicating an excess of excuses? Over-explaining keeps us exceedingly stuck, expounding on the extraneous, exterior circumstances. In contrast, embracing experiences provides feedback.

What can be expected when we extinguish our own power and put our expectations on others? Expecting someone or something else to change is an expectation that solutions should be external. Unless, of course, you've already decided to just exchange it or them for a better model.

We've all exhibited less-than-excellent examples, reacting with exasperation when someone or something didn't meet our so-called reasonable expectations or, worse, exhibited unexpressed reflections of ourselves we'd prefer to exclude.

Besides, expectations set us up for premeditated resentment.

Pre-meditated. By the way, did you meditate before you decided to embrace that resentment? No? So, now you're being re-sent back to a resentful state of mind? Hmm. Re-minder time?

Imagine extracting yourself and others from the burden of expectation. We create meaningful exchanges when we don't give any ex too much power. The rate exchange for guilt is far too expensive, so expend your excess in gentle examination. You didn't really know what to expect except based on your past story of how it *should* go. Exonerate them, and yourself.

Let's be existential examples for one another. Consider replacing your expectations with embracing your own heartfelt, empowering expressions of awareness, authenticity, acceptance, and alignment. Ask for an exceptional perspective; then, from *that* mindset, act.

Exalt the present moment. Extra-curricular learning expands us, so . . .

Excogitate. (Contemplate.) Expiate. (Compensate.)

You are always the expert in your experience. You are the one who was there, then.

You are the one who is here, now. Observe what's going on inside your body, mind, heart, and spirit.

Delight in exposing the exotic, extraordinary, and exceptional expression that exists in that expansive mind of yours.

Excited? Excellent!

Stay alert in the wisdom of now. Follow the energy of what brings you back to your joy, your essence, your sense of connection. Experiment with the experiential. Remember that divinely downloaded message you received a few years ago? Here's what it said: Experience the Eternal in the Eternal Experience.

— *G.O.D. Journals, September 2014*

DO THE DAMN EXERCISES

Maybe you, like me, habitually skipped over the exercise section of every self-help book. Geeze, even *skipping over* sounds like exercise. But hey, if you are tempted to go there now, hold on just a sec and at least scan this section.

I've always loved attending seminars and workshops. Perhaps taking the term *self-help* a little too seriously, I was assistance addicted but action avoidant. An appreciative hunter-gatherer, perhaps I latently lamented that excessive notetaking exonerated me from practical practice.

For much of my adult life, I hated looking in the mirror, physically and metaphorically. Habitually blocking any semblance of self-compassion, I nearly always centered my focus around excess weight. No surprise, with Ms. Judgment constantly on my back.

Habitually avoiding all forms of exercise, I excused myself, bemoaning how such exercitations *made me* uncomfortable, which seemed easier than owning the extensive discomfort within.

Bottom line: My inner rebel just didn't freakin' feel like doing the work.

Suffering protects our victim role, a strategy that significantly exterminates access to authenticity. Expending endless energy in expression repression, we won't see our bandages as bandits, robbing us from our essence. Perhaps we fear lead exposure, knowing, at some level, something is leading us forward, calling forth our inner leader, whispering, "You, too, have something to bring."

> Embrace that which truly brings you the experience of clarity, peace of mind, and purpose. Invest there. Everything else is avoidance. There is a delicate dance between being and doing. It is wonderfully important to sit in meditation and contemplation, yet insights must be brought into action to be shared, to grow, to expand. Avoiding action results in contraction (contra-action!). Taking the risk to move forward in small steps results in an ever-widening expansion onto new pathways into possibility.
>
> *— G.O.D. Journals, August 2015*

Inevitably, though, awareness of patterns does emerge. Perhaps part of the purpose of those lifechanging workshops was to morph my obliviousness into the obvious. From an overt inner space of almost obnoxious obsequiousness to obdurate objection, I observed my opinion of those revered leaders snap my shift right back into my shit. Starry-eyed admiration turned to inner sighs and consternation at the drop of their blissful announcement:

"So, let's do an exercise!"

Uh-oh. Survival mind kicks in, pretending it's not.

Wait, what, work? At a workshop? That's stupid! Why? Exerting effort requires too much exertion and effort! Hide out, sit this one out! Okay, I know, I'll run to my car. By the time I gulp down a can of caffeinated soda, go to the bathroom, I'll get back just in time to hear all about how great the exercise was — for others.

The extradited expat victim that lived within was being pulled away from familiar territory. In process of exposure, there was a subconscious urge for momentum, to risk something new, becoming an exchange student of sorts. While odd chants continued to skip through my unconsciousness — that probably sounded something like: *Teeska, tooska, I'm tiring of tears, but still so ashamed, and so many fears* — I couldn't help but notice another inner Persy impatiently cranking the rope. She was sorely up to her neck in sore arms, getting crankier by the moment, waiting for me to freakin' get over myself, and just jump in. Was it really so hard to drop the rope of the inner tug-of-war? Geesh.

Ego takes one more stab: *Just leave! You have all the notes. Besides, you know damn well you'll never look at them again, anyway. Nothing ever changes, especially not you.*

Choosing the extemporaneous over extinguishment is the beginning of a new exposé. Grudgingly, I heeded the urge to emerge; to trust the path of trudge, one exertion at a time. Admittedly, though, attitude altitude is a steep climb. Assimilation takes time, as does ass-elimination. Embracing exemplary exemplification, I stepped into a future knowing: My work was meant to become my play.

Risk being wrong about your coveted fairytales while learning to trust. Take actions you've never tried before. Embark on a whole new level. Constantly checking for intangible signs of change is a piss-poor prerequisite prior to recognizing tangible results. Pretend to have faith, even when you can't yet see that something exciting is expanding.

The only one who needs to see and hear you is you. Explore your inner fitness room. Be kind to the one in the mirror. No one, not even you, gets to judge. Still, enlist the support of safe and healthy neutral parties as you see (and get) fit. Get experiential, as you experience exhilaration.

So, let's do an exercise!

This exercise of listening while writing is designed to increase your muscle of Awareness. Continue distinguishing between the voices and mindsets you are choosing. Observe the differences. No matter how far you scatter, you are still part of the same Energy that created you. Keep connecting with Source. Let the rest fall away, so you see heaven is already here.

— *G.O.D. Journals, January 2012*

REMEMBER STRAIGHT-A STRATEGIES TO EMBRACE ANY EX

Discover what, where, when, and with whom you notice exceptions, excitement, exclusions, excellence, exhaustion, calls for expansion, ex-cetera. And yes, I know the word is actually *etcetera*, but the exaltation of creativity over formality shall serve as my exculpation.

> *Awareness.* Mindfulness. Your mind is full, but of what? Are they thoughts you opt to keep? What is inviting deeper examination, draining or driving your energy? Exercise this moment's opportunity to examine what is exacting your attention.

- *Authenticity.* Exercise can be painful when overdone, so create a healthy environment. Thoughts and feelings entrapped in the mind and body need appropriate acknowledgment. Render them powerless to keep you unconsciously ensnared within your story. Experiment with various harmless methods or media of creative expression, for example, movement, arts and crafts, collage, writing, clay.
- *Acceptance.* Does letting go of judgment seem too extreme? When resisting acceptance, something's keeping you stuck. Check in. What exceptions are ruling? Have you any unrealistic expectations? You may be exhausted. You might need to exhale. Explore, explore, explore.
- *Alignment.* You're in the middle of a major exercise session, building new muscle. Whether you're breaking down, breaking up, or breaking through, it's okay to take a break. How's your heart rate? Take a breath; it's breathtaking. Do you need some water? Cool-down time? Normalizing new ways of thinking and being often feels like vigorous exercise: both energizing and exhausting.
- *Ask.* Exercise requires staying on track and open to feedback from your being. Set down any physical, emotional, mental, or metaphoric weight. Release the heaviness of irrational expectations you've trained yourself to carry. Feel relief in momentary relaxation. Inhale. Stay there. Exhale. Listen for your next direction. How is your Inner Informant informing you?
- *Action.* You're in action, right now. You're doing the damn exercise! You didn't even have to physically move if you didn't want to. See how life plays out while working itself out?

Thoughts and emotions entrapped in the mind and body will keep energy ensnared within the story, so why not play with exploring safe and simple ways to express the unexpressed? Write out whatever's been writhing within, then host a private tearing and tearing session! Go ahead, cry it out, then rip 'em to pieces! Collage that mirage! Dance out your stance! Punch a pile of clay until it portrays your rage! Hell, draw the craw out of your jaw, then paint the pain right out of your brain!

Enjoy experimenting with expelling—while exercising your right—and the delight—found in exorcising your authentic, yet momentary, experience. Exercises in self-care exude exhilaration. Expression is the expressway to healing.

This is a now life, based on this moment's action to create your future. You aren't waiting for Me, because *I AM* in the Now. You say you are waiting for you, but aren't you already here too? Already is different from being all-ready. Your mind will try to convince you: You aren't ready. But you won't ever be ready if you are never here, will you? What part of you are you waiting for? You see, Love, the Love Energy is already here. It always has been, always will be. In all ways. Embrace this idea, integrate it. It is really quite simple, if you are willing.

— *G.O.D Journals, June 2012*

EXTRA CREDIT EXERCISE EXPERIENCES!

Play with these statements to promote extra self-awareness. Let *x* represent any perception you currently are holding of yourself. Look for patterns, stories, and ways of being from that particular mindset, then examine new possibilities, perhaps from a more supportive viewpoint.

Example: *When I perceive myself as* x *then, I:*

- Get to . . . *x*
- Don't get to . . . *x*
- Have to . . . *x*
- Don't have to . . . *x*

Existential inquiry. Make it up any way you want. Play with different perspectives. Stay attuned to those expressive stories or songs you habitually tell or sing to yourself, so you'll know if it's time to change your tune.

- Which unmet expectations get in your way?
- What experiment can you create, just to observe the experience?
- Where in life are you afraid of exposure? Expansion?
- Who or what exhausts you? Anything or anyone you need to expel?
- What excites your sense of purpose? What step will you take to embrace that?

Let go of pretending to know. Your judgment or opinion of a situation does not make it so. It's merely a temporary state of mind, and therefore, meaningless. Exercise your willingness and innate ability to rise above human thinking. Choose to welcome in My Guidance. Demonstrate the reality of My presence and permanence within.

— *G.O.D. Journals, October 2015*

CHAPTER 14

the end game

You already have all the information and direction you need for your next steps. The opportunity is to mindfully choose. There is no need to be attached to outcome, for it is only in the actual experience of being present in the Presence you will know. Breathe in the Loving that is You. Gift it everywhere.

— G.O.D. Journals, August 2015

NONRESISTANCE TO YOUR EXISTENCE

Stop resisting your existence. Awareness of struggle is only a signpost, a place to pause along the way when your energy is waning. Wherever you've landed, you might as well check out the curios and discover what's inside. Take a look, but remember, buying is optional. Feel free to ignore any annoying inner salesclerks who might have an agenda.

Thanks, just looking.

By noticing what's in store, you're honoring what's here. Imagine you are a funky junk shop, with antiquities galore. What treasures are hiding in those dusty corners? Check in with inner inquiry. Is this item worth picking up? Should you invest your time, investigate further? Or is it just more crap you no longer have use for? Tune in. What's your body telling you? Your mind? Your emotions?

Child, even your meandering, judgmental thoughts are part of your pathway home, for they, too, lead you back to Me. Judging them simply takes you further down their path, which is fine, if that's the route you choose to take. But you will return to Me.

— *G.O.D. Journals, July 2014*

I'm guessing I'm not alone in experiencing a sense of being in complete alignment with Guidance, then a split-second later, doubting it even exists. There's an awkward dance between recognition and resistance, a perpetual invitation to move out of the familiar into the unknown, then back again. A self-conscious sashay, being led by a Creator beyond my understanding.

Breathe a sigh of relief, knowing you are back on track. Drop the debate, the debunked debacle that you can ever make a once-and-for-all decision. Instead, choose in the present, as you learn to practice building trust with your default decider. Do you want a mindset that bases its conclusions on temporary external circumstances, or consistent internal experience?

Accept the invitation to listen for what you need to know, just for now. Risk trusting that Guidance is always in process of revealing Itself. Embrace the idea of being at peace with the idea of having no idea. You don't yet know how, when, or in what form your Guidance will appear. But appear, It will.

Let the unknown be what it is: unknown.

Each experience of noticing the inner battles, limiting beliefs, attachments to misery, the inevitable disappointments of the lower mind, is here for your growth. Be a conscious, consistent part of a divine experiment, with fun and joy. The outcome is already assured. There are no fixes, only your fixations. Have I not shown you, time and again, I have only your highest good in mind? Embrace, experience, the loving that is always here. Is it not easier and more fun to just relax and let Me show you the way? I can use everything, if only you are willing to let Me.

— *G.O.D. Journals, July 2014*

BYOB: BE YOUR OWN BESTIE

Bring to mind a life-changing moment. You know, one in which you heard something so profound you couldn't quite decide if it was terrible news or a great relief. Sound familiar? Yes, indeed, we did travel down that eucalyptus-scented path together, as we prepared to enter this particular playground of profundity.

Sensible or nonsensical, this segment of our journey together now seems to be coming to completion. Integrating my own awareness as this final chapter unfolds, in full-frontal fashion, I must humbly confess, I wrote this book for me.

I knew it was necessary to examine my patterns of endless searching. Attempts to find *the way* in ways that continually resonated was my unconscious way to direct and control the show. Yet this adventure continues to show me that it's me alone who gets in the way of the Direction the Director is showing. Musing me right back into humbling, mumbling mulling, I gotta wonder, could it be that every perceived beginning—and ending—is divinely designed to be recognized as an endearing escapade into That Which Is Endless?

Errors in perception do nothing to change reality. They simply change the narrative. Maybe the whole reason we exist is to practice being in divine partnership with Source. With ever-increasing frequency, you, too, may be feeling that desire to co-create from your ephemeral authenticity, demonstrating Spirit's infinite forms of finite expression.

So, delight in discovering your unique ways to embrace your talents and your triggers while playfully imagining the profound impacts your co-creations could create. By continuing to fulfill our self-sacrificing call to service, maybe in the process we'll learn to sacrifice our pesky aversion to self-forgiveness.

Perhaps the thread or dread that weaves us together is the profound realization of just how much one's authentic sharing contributes to the healing of the whole. Relief returns every time I am gifted the reassurance that I am not alone. And yet, I am still apparently required to contend with the contention of my ego, who thrives on unhealthy competition. I guess there remains a fearful part inside who is convinced another's newfound invulnerability will somehow undermine or invalidate my own.

You never know when you will make a lasting impression, but what's impressive is this: The lasting impression we make upon ourselves is based on the moment-by-moment choices of how we see ourselves. So, consider impressing upon yourself the following realities:

- No one will ever understand you better than you. Let go of what others think. Be you.
- No one speaks, listens, or hears you more than you do. Be kind. Be honest.
- You are the only one who will always be with you. Sorry, but you really can't get away from your *self*, nor, thankfully, your *Self.* Learn to discern between the two.
- Let go of your existing, exhausting self-judgment. Find something to celebrate instead.
- No one else has the power to *make you* do or be anything. Embrace your Inner Guidance.
- Your dreams are yours. What you do with them is up to you.
- Your profound way of being, who you choose to be, in this moment, influences every choice you make and will have an impact on everyone you meet.

No matter where you are in your journey, let it be okay. Self-acceptance is the key. Your best friend has been with you all along—and always will be.

Isn't it time you acknowledge them?

When you are aware that you have forgotten, you have remembered. Don't beat yourself up for forgetting, rather, celebrate that you have remembered. Listen. Self-forgiveness is always your Guiding Light back to Me.

— *G.O.D. Journals, January 2012*

BFF – BE FORGIVING OF FORGETTING

You're the only one 100 percent guaranteed to be with you the rest of your life.

Why not get to know your perceptions, problems, and perfectionistic tendencies? Learn to interplay with all your quirky peeps inside, perceiving each as a potential pointer toward profundity. Imagine automatically loving all of life, and all of you; being all here, all in, and all the time.

Being eternally pro-found, you can't lose yourself. But in order to live in profundity, you'll be required to accept all of who you are. After all, the role of a best friend is best played by one who encourages, upholds, and champions our most revered qualities while fearlessly providing frank feedback as needed. Carefrontation.

We spend endless time uselessly searching, don't we? Pro-found, con-found, we all get so doggone attached to our confounded story, it keeps us from getting (or forgetting) our unique profundity. Although none of us are designed to design another's inner journey, surely, we'll intertwine. Thankfully, it's our distinct inner differences—not our indifferences—that make such a difference in the outer world.

Alas, you'll probably find yourself getting caught up, at least one more time, in old habits. Those mischievous little mindsets of fear, guilt, and judgment can be as stubborn as the stubbornness that dreads their demise. It's almost as if human nature rebels, insisting our peace of mind must be pursued via external extremes. Yet release creates increase. Foregoing what no longer fulfills means more space to expand and explore. Alternatives abound.

Find forgiveness challenging? Maybe that's because Ms. Understanding and Ms. Giving are hovering nearby, standing in their fundamental misunderstandings and misgivings.

Habitually holding onto self-righteous resentments, grudges, and self-disparagement, they beg us to piously plead for mercy upon our souls.

But what if every misgiving is also a gift, here for-our-giving?

Admittedly, the trouble often lies in a faulty receiver. So, let's complicate matters further, and add a receivership clause: For something to be sincerely given, it must have a humble receiver. But while we are eternally entangled in unconscious, self-conscious self-condemnation while condemning another, we furtively fear forgiveness is fully fallacious, and therefore futile.

If we can't receive it, how the hell can we authentically give it? No wonder we don't get it. Forget it. Yeah, I know it's late in the game, but here we are, back to *F it!*

It is okay that you forget, as I will always lead you back. You have come a long way, from active resistance to intentional remembering, and everything in between. Working by yourself provides growth opportunities, but why choose the painful path of judgment, frustration, and ineffective use of time? Learning to work with Me is your play, joy, and growth. Let your life be an adventure.

— *G.O.D. Journals, August 2020*

Consider the inner space you might create simply by releasing a few of your most toxic attack thoughts. Previously occupied by preoccupations, you've just made a little more room for Guidance to be received. Forgive yourself. Uncover what's waiting for you. Align with receivership. Alternatives abound, remember?

So, again I ponder: What if everything is here for-our-getting, and for-our-giving? Let's stop getting distracted by the divergent dichotomies that plague us. Unconsciously holding a thought as *thou-ought* only adds more guilt. Notice the word *ugh* conveniently intertwined in the mess. If thou art forgiving because thou *ought*, art thou not creating thine own inauthenticity?

What is it you want to get? Are you *for* getting it? Will you bring it? To be fair, seems you must be equally committed to be *for*-giving and *for*-getting whatever it is you wish to receive.

If you haven't been for-giving, does that mean you were against giving what you want?

I didn't think so. Forgive yourself.

You just forgot to practice trusting your path and Guidance.

Who better to remind you of what you really want than your own, omnipresent BFF? When you bring your own bestie (BYOB) to life's daily party, you are consciously reminding yourself your best friend forever (BFF) will always be by your side, gently whispering omnipresent reminders of exactly who you aspire to be in this very moment. You bring with you your comfort, your joy; all the qualities you wish to give to others, while gracefully remaining aware of the insightful gifts they are bringing you.

Like Santa, your Inner Guidance knows when you've tired of your own arrested development. A tiny breath of conscious surrender is all It needs. Now practice patiently waiting in the receiving room of your mind, where your gift of inner peace is sure to be soon delivered.

Knowing and experiencing My Guidance is always available to anyone who is truly willing, but the ego mind is full of itself. Emptying it out will make room for Me. Do not fear your fearful thoughts, for that gives them power. Face them with others you trust, and you will be contributing to the healing of minds and hearts untold.

— *G.O.D. Journals, September 2020*

FROM WHY'S TO WISE

Ever feel powerless over your thoughts, as if they were choosing you? When we play the victim card of unawareness, we might be tempted to fume inside ourselves. *They make me so . . .* or, *It's because . . .* or, *I can't help how I feel!* I mean, why take responsibility for my inner experience when I can find someone or something to blame? Why, indeed?

If you seem to be losing your mind, it's a sign to get out of your head. Getting lost in thy sacred *why's* hides your wise one inside. Generally speaking, *why* questions aren't so profound. Unlikely to provide the true answers you seek, endless *why* queries can be equated to inviting the universe to send you yet another shitload shipment of unverifiable upsets. Like retail therapy at the dollar store, you'll end up with more crap you'll never use.

Don't get me wrong. Questioning ourselves helps us discover where our wisdom lives. But stay aware of the quality of the questioner, and its possible agenda to obtain elusive answers. What does it hope to find? Your True Self will not demand you go without; rather, it will encourage you to commandeer courageous moments to go within.

Invoke your divine imagination which is always at your service. Ask it to help you co-create a wise Inner Council. Have fun. Make it up any way you want. Who will you put on your board of directors? What qualities do they embody? In what ways do they reflect whom you aspire to be? Just be sure you choose directors who are at least a little wiser than your inner wise guy. You want mentors who see through your self-deprecating delusions—and aren't afraid to say so.

What do they know about you that you are ready to accept in yourself? What honest feedback can they offer? Go ahead, ask them. Yes. Now.

Knowing the qualities you bring, they call you forward, advocating for your talents, compassion, and joyful service while calling you out on the thoughts that hold you back. Right in the midst of your for-getting and for-giving, they stand with you, knowing you want nothing more than to generously share all the wisdom you've received on your journey. Pun-fully appropriate, consider seating an older, wiser version of yourself as—and on—your chair.

After all, remember: Nobody knows you better than You. Sit with that. And them.

Your highest thoughts about yourself and others will continue to arise and evolve, if you let them. Recognize infinity by uncovering and releasing that which is finite and perishable. Relax in the delight, beauty, and miracles of growth simply by shedding what no longer serves. As forms change, they serve in new ways. Rejoice in your service today, Child. The energy of All That Is—is already within all that is.

— *G.O.D. Journals, May 2015*

UNDISCIPLINED DISCIPLE

Unlearning takes serious self-discipline, but we needn't take ourselves so seriously. Playing with profundity implies we are pro-fun, right? When life seems to be falling apart, Guidance shows us how to put it back together in profound new ways. But that entails letting go of control—stepping away from stories we know so well.

The word *discipline* used to trigger me, thinking I had to do something I had no energy or desire to do. That is, until one blessed day, I misread it as *disciple*. In a momentous shame reframe, a shift in seeing became a shift in being; habitual distractibility, humble teachability. What if everything is an opportunity to refocus, re-minders we're on the way to our next nexus?

If you, too, tend to lack discipline, with just a little willingness and humility, you can always ask your G.O.D., and your BFF, to support you in finding profound new ways to connect with your profundity—that which has been waiting to connect with you.

What might happen if you decided to forgo those fears you've been treasuring? Fearlessly finding out might require playing with the projections in your periphery.

Note the similarities between the characters in your mind and those who show up in your world. Observe their personas, strategies, and manifestations. What about them do you love? Pour energy into that. What parts of them annoy you? Pull back your perception, park it in neutrality. How, when, why, and with whom are you just like them?

Noticing the battle while no longer choosing the fight is how we win the war.

Signs, signals, metaphors, and messages are everywhere. Nature, chance encounters, triggers, trash. Dreams, songs, advertisements, bumper stickers, license plates, billboards.

The more present you are, the more potential for fun—and encouragement—to keep on playing. Dig for your treasures if you must, but maybe you needn't work so hard.

Your inner and outer space adventure will surely bring needed clues. You hold the power to reinvent any and all parts of yourself. Previously unowned energies, renowned and renewed, are instantly available to join Team Profundity.

Disciplined by momentary awareness, become teachable. A disciple for truth. Authenticity points the way to acceptance and transcendence. From a mindset of service, our most challenging situations align as we ask for, then activate, the momentum into awareness of the higher realms.

Have faith in something other than your own default thinking. Prioritize spending time with that which inspires you. Check in with those who encourage you to keep on checking in with your ever-evolving inspired self. Trust that the disciplines you choose today are preparing you for your role in divine discipleship tomorrow.

Go to that place in your mind where only peace resides. See the beauty, hear the harmony, experience the heaven on earth already within you; awake, alive, ready to be born. Bring that presence into the world, and listen:
You fear it is too difficult
To hear the words I speak
Yet discipline, devotion
Gives the only gift you seek
You're challenged by commitment
As lower mind defends

Yet discipline, devotion
Watches mind as it transcends
Creating from a higher realm
Acknowledge Creator's thought
As Disciple and Devoted
Experience what you sought.
Tune in. Trust. Take Action. You are already ready, as you always have been, for whatever is in front of you. I will never be angry or demanding with you, but I will be direct. Ah yes, could that be why we are calling this your Guided Omnipresent Direction?

— G.O.D. Journals, March 2016

UNIVERSAL TUITION

Perhaps there's no mistake that the word *university* roots itself in *universe*. I just heard my inner spiritual bypass surgeon tsk-tsking: *Of course, there are no mistakes!* Under the loving direction of one Creator, let's surmise there is at least one universal lesson plan worth repeating: Love and accept yourself. Extend that same courtesy to every other being.

The mounting cost of using our time here to strategize against our biggest rival, The Fighting Egos, is just not sustainable. Opposition is exhausting; it no longer fits the playbook.

Alas, surrender. The price of an Earth-school education.

The tuition we pay to be here isn't earmarked for subsidizing fear, irritation, worries, or obsessions. Our borrowed time is up. The price to keep repeating the same curricula has become unaffordable. Fortunately, Universal University won't kick us out. Still, it's time to be responsible, pay off our student loans, utilizing both loan- and self-forgiveness. Now's the only time to pay forward that which we intuitively need to integrate.

The curriculum can change quickly, so stay present in your current lesson plan. And if you aren't sure who or what that entails, take the time for both recess and reassessment. Invite challenges, self-criticism, and vulnerabilities to transform into your superpowers. Play. Get messy. Mess with whatever's messing with you. Insist your I-don't-know-how voice shows its hallowed know-how.

Practice professing your innate wisdom. Access that In-Tuition, that Inner Teacher, that Inner Teen. Whatever you choose to call your I.T., just call it. Higher Power, G.O.D., Jesus, Buddha, Presence, Loving Inner Parent, Great Spirit, BFF . . . no matter. It knows Who you mean. What *does* matter is the regular renewal of your willingness to re-cognize to the part of your Mind that is ready, available and accessible, to assist you, right now.

What could be more fun than dedicating one's life to demonstrating the relief found in being real? With nothing to hide (from yourself!) you'd literally be carefree. Bring your gifts everywhere. Prepare for a whole new career.

Ever consider becoming a heavenly host?

Imagine being unmoved by outer drama, rather, being moved by inner dharma. Imagine you and your fellow beings consciously connecting with all higher selves, guided and moved by a universal mindset of service, each in your own special way. Bringing Creator Mind everywhere, you'll cultivate an inner plot as to how you can best co-create heaven on earth.

Guidance is a gift. Your tuition is pre-paid; it is part of the package deal that came with you on this Earth-school adventure. Stay alert, teachable, ready for those inner promptings. Lessons come in endless forms. Remain calm and compassionate with yourself as you automatically, intuitively, teach the love you've learned, in the way only you can do.

You feel connected, grounded, safe when you follow your intuition, your inspiration. In-tuition: Inner-education. Inspiration: Inner-spirit. Trusting Me is only challenging when you won't. Then you suffer as a result. Suffering is not necessary or beneficial; it is a learned behavior, a defense, habit, survival. Release the fear of finding what is underneath.

— *G.O.D. Journals, October 2014*

IT'S UP TO U-N-I

Ever experience a fleeting moment of joyous relief, realizing that maybe you weren't in charge after all? You can never be disconnected from That Which Created You.

Imagine if you truly accepted everything as a part of yourself. Consider this: Every form of Creation must have ultimately come from a Master Creator. Who or What created this Universe? From planets to plants, how the heaven did they manage to plant themselves where they are? Who accrued the right elements to procure a miraculous cure, and what ensured their way to do so?

It stands to reason that the loving energy through which Creation constantly creates must be alive and well within us all. And accessible. In what ways are *you* being called to demonstrate this must be so, so you can integrate, then demonstrate, that Knowledge?

Profound callings continually call, waiting for our acknowledgment. Choosing to regularly reconnect with that co-creative part of your being is a commitment to consciously connect with whatever creations you are destined to bring.

Think of it this way: Those of us who still regularly get lost in our own for-getting profoundly want to get—to receive—that which is created for-giving. I know, it sounds convoluted, but it really isn't. Try thinking of *forgiving* as *for-healing*. Forgiveness heals.

Bottom line: Your elixir is another's fixer. Someone's innocent laughter might trigger another's disaster, but what if even that calamity was meant to eventually contribute to all of humanity?

In my playful world, the work must start from the inside out. Maybe you, too, are feeling the urgent need to finally face your shit, so you can finally embrace your shift.

And share it.

After all, it is all about U.

Understanding all parts of ourselves is an undertaking equal to taking a stand for our innocent underlings. When it's time to undo something, you might need to ask parts of yourself to stand aside while you stand still in your unrelenting Higher Mind. Replace unawareness with unfolding silent direction, uninhabited by the world's chatter. Unchain yourself. Untether that unconditional love you bring.

Unity, conveniently embedded in the words *opportunity* and *community*, will always begin with U 'n' I. Let's trust our Guidance. Even when we are all-but-for-getting our Direction, know the time will come when we will be all-for-giving it.

What if you knew, without a doubt, you were here for a purpose, even if you didn't yet know what that purpose was? What would you do that you aren't doing now? What would you stop doing that you are doing now?

— *G.O.D. Journals, January 2015*

THE ETERNAL PLAY

Hey, do you believe in predestination?

You might remember that I do. Our paths must have been destined to intertwine, in this eternal moment known as *time*.

Here on this shared playground called *life*—where the Heart, Mind, Wisdom, and Source of all Creation play right alongside us—entertaining enlightenment awaits. Noticing the energies, stories, and patterns that perpetually play themselves through us offers the gift of insight through hindsight.

Yet with no endgame in sight, what choice do we truly have or desire but to play life forward, while practicing being exactly who we want to be?

Your Creator created you like Itself. Let It reveal Itself to you in ways only you will recognize. Become willing to focus on the brilliance inherent in *all* of creation. Bask in the knowing that, somehow, whatever is before you, be-here, *for* you. Be present, open the gift. Step out of your story and into your life.

Perhaps our only job is to embrace the eternal opportunity to listen for and act upon the gentle loving Guidance we receive. For some of us, that might require responding to a not-so-subtle summons:

Put pen to paper—and listen.

You'll never know when you'll be called upon to share a story about a wee-hour call you received. Speaking from experience, sometimes it's more than two decades later.

And there might be a time when those calls for your cooperation come with specific intuitive instructions, such as:

Utilize a noncapitalized letter 'i.'
Acknowledging your small-self mindset is part of the healing process.

Apparently, there's just no point in trying to go back to sleep.

The Eternal Play

Peace
i cease
Now Spirit is released, to
heal
and reveal
The love that's underneath, a
veil
of hell
Wants only to be parted, to
end
or transcend
This play that never started, stage
fright
i might
accept another sight, That
Sees
with ease
Dark dissolving into light, yet
resistance
i distance
From that Voice of insistence, Who
Knows
What flows
From the Source of all existence

264

Sigh
Sob-cry
Surrender and just die, to
no worry
now hurry
to the place where I will fly, into
Peace
i cease
Now Spirit is released, to . . .

Channeled Poetry, June 15, 2005, 3:30 a.m.

It seems everything is designed for our awakening. Often, quite literally.
You are the One you have been waiting for.

Embrace the eternal. Play with your profundity. There's no need to keep searching.
You've already arrived.

AFTERWORD

There's always more to say, but need I?

No surprise here. Writing my first afterword is triggering me. Another divine opportunity to call myself forward, sans the blessed distraction of the pun power I enjoyed way back when I wrote my first foreword.

One of my favorite quotes from *A Course in Miracles* is: "Let us not forget, however, that words are but symbols of symbols. They are thus twice removed from reality" (ACIM 2007). Whoa. Reality. My ego wants to fight me on this, but Silence beholds my greatest teacher. Moving beyond this wordy world, listening brings me back home.

The ongoing direction to take responsibility for whatever upsets must be a divine setup, demanding I practice what I preach. Fortunately, I recently noticed I need only take apart, then rearrange, the letters in the word *practice* — and voilà! *Cite crap*.

Inundating oneself with endless *why's* just evades the eventual and inevitable yielding to the wiser voice inside. Maybe the meltdown muse is meant to protect that child who's never quite sure of what they're doing, since finishing one project means facing the fear of not knowing whatever the hell is next, let alone if they'll be able to handle it. But here's where awareness comes in handy. Stay caught in dramatics and semantics, or choose a solution that brings peace of mind.

Maybe there is no afterword; only the continual call to trust, to move toward one's calling, to stay aware of our stuff. Make it a playful, entertaining habit. You know, *HA! BIT!* Laugh a bit. Cry . . . a lot. Ask for Guidance. Be willing to receive it.

Little by little, piece by piece, we playfully make peace with all the bits and pieces within our treasured selves. So, thanks for sticking around, Dear Reader. Risking sharing my awarenesses with you (*Reality check:* sharing them with myself) *is* my solution. Here's to real-izing, once again, we're never alone. Guidance will always be right here, patiently awaiting our willingness to return home.

NEXUS PERPLEXUS

Playing with profundity is an ongoing adventure to behold, so why not check in with your Inner Guidance right now, and melodically inquire, "What's ready to unfold?"

Pro Tip: Now, speaking from experience, the playful trick is to practice patience while listening for your authentic answers. Remember, if we rearrange *practice* we can see it as *cite crap*. Reassure the part inside who tends to collapse into "I dunno." Just don't let that part of you retreat into the stench of prolonged stagnation. Let courage counterbalance any concerns. A new now is always presenting itself.

Ever have the feeling some*one* or some*thing* just *gets* you? You may have felt that way while listening to a piece of music, or gazing at an art piece, or —*ahem*— reading a book. You might have intuitively felt seen, heard, in a way heretofore unknown. You might have even felt a bit intimidated, knowing you wanted more, but of what, you weren't quite sure.

So just how does inner darkness become outer light? Ultimately, that's up to you.

Some of the most difficult and profound choices I have made involved a willingness to ask for a conversation with someone I felt naturally drawn toward. Sensing opportunities for growth, to move beyond the great beyond of my unknowing, I began to cite my own crap and practice risking, and eventually trusting, transformation.

So hey, whether this book was a help or a hinderance, I hope you uncovered a hidden treasure or two. A little bit of shift—even when, or especially if, it momentarily looks like shit—is here to contribute to your growth, as long as you are willing to see or seed it that way.

If you are considering working with a trusted partner to accompany you on your inner space adventure, I can't encourage you enough to get to know that Still Small Voice inside; that One that knows what's best for you at this point in your life.

Should you feel called to find out how we might journey together for a spell, please consider exploring my website at mariannewagner.com/coaching.

Whatever you feel called to do or say, you have my support. I'd love to hear from you. Feel free to send a note to mariannewagner.com/contact or visit my website, authentically.be.

REFERENCES

ACIM. 2007. *A Course in Miracles*, Third Edition, copyright © 2007 by the Foundation for Inner Peace, copyright holder and publisher, 448 Ignacio Blvd., #306, Novato, CA 94949, acim.org. (M–21.1:9–10).

To learn more about A Course in Miracles, please visit the website of the scribe-authorized publisher and copyright holder of the Course, the Foundation for Inner Peace (www.acim.org). The Foundation for Inner Peace, a nonprofit organization, has been dedicated to publishing, distributing, and discussing A Course in Miracles since 1975.

ACKNOWLEDGMENTS

First, a toast to our shared creative Creator! As we each bring forth our little piece of heaven on earth, may we experience that divine co-creative energy coming through us as unconditional love, understanding, compassion, and joyous laughter.

I am incredibly grateful for the ongoing Guidance that comes in endless forms and always right on time. Particularly influential on my journey have been teachings from *A Course in Miracles*, Unity, Centers for Spiritual Living; the Spiritual Psychology Programs through the University of Santa Monica and the 12 Step rooms of recovery. In addition, the transformational support I have received from the amazing folks at Seshat Press has been invaluable.

I am, of course, most grateful for my immediate family.

A special thanks—and apologies—to my hubby, Gary. Who knew, over forty-six years ago, what an adventure we would share? Despite my dramatic lamentations about how much I would hate to be married to me, thus keeping my ego both the center of attention and the victim, I am eternally grateful for your loving support. Your caring heart, appreciation for nature, and tireless demonstration of perseverance in times of challenge are inspirational gifts to all you encounter. Thank you for reminding us to take it easy and to stop and smell the roses, even when those damn thorns poke us in sensitive places. You are love, loved, and I love you.

My daughter, Brianna, my forever-preferred partner in mischievous conduct—and reality checks. It's no wonder the meaning of your name includes qualities such as *brilliance* and *strength*. Your creative marketing, tech, and proofreading skills, combined with your forthright way of being and natural tendency to champion and encourage, have proven to be invaluable throughout this adventure. Our relationship is, I am sure, a divine demonstration in the power of intentional healing. May we stand together in mom-mending throughout millennia, mesmerized by miracles made manifest. Moo-Moo loves you!

My extraordinary son, Nathaniel, has always been a player with profundity. As your name implies, I knew from the moment you were conceived, you were a gift from God. A genuine genius in your own right, you are an amazing dad with a compassionate heart and a musically mystical mind. Your keen awareness and sensitivity toward nature, your talent for writing and wordplay, combined with the ability to maintain a wacky sense of humor during times of challenge, provide authentic, inspired insight to everyone you touch. I love you, Nateson.

Somewhere along the line, our little family must have made a pact to break the unconscious rules and patterns of generations of family dysfunction. In the process, we created our own. I am forever grateful to know we are always here for one another. To infinity, and beyond!

Last but not least, I want to acknowledge every member of my extended human family. Be we friends, fellow travelers, or former foes, each of you have served in significant ways along my journey. Isn't it wonderful to know we're always led to our divine right peeps? If you've been in my life—past, present, or future—for a moment or a millennium, you've influenced my journey.

Without each of your contributions, this book never would have manifested. We all call each other forward, somehow mirroring each other's madness and magnificence. May our individual healings continue to be miraculous catalysts for every other life we touch.

ABOUT THE AUTHOR

Quickly approaching her seventh decade, Marianne K. Wagner grew up in a metaphysically minded, but emotionally intolerant, alcoholic home. A highly sensitive, socially awkward, overweight kid, she considers herself extremely fortunate to have grown up during the Love Generation of the 1960s, in the artistically oriented, free-thinking town of Laguna Beach, California.

Before the age of ten, Marianne first felt the thrill of becoming a published author. Having risked entering her poetry in a weekly kids' contest put on by a local newspaper, her original rhymes garnered, on more than one occasion, the coveted first prize of a Kennedy half-dollar.

During her late teens and early twenties she earned an associate of arts degree and a certificate in early childhood education. Marianne became a devoted preschool teacher for twelve years while concurrently uncovering a playful child within.

By her mid-twenties, Marianne was noticing the nudges toward a shift in lifestyle. Unexpectedly connecting with angelic agents of change, she accepted support from mentors, counselors, and fellow travelers in the 12-Step rooms of recovery. Though food and body struggles remain a daily challenge, Marianne holds deep gratitude for over forty continuous years of sobriety from alcohol and recreational drugs.

Employed by a local municipality for over two decades, Marianne grew increasingly aware of patterns—in herself, family, friends, coworkers, and clients—that stirred an unstoppable longing to heal the misunderstandings of the past. By her mid-thirties, she found herself in the depths of a dark night of the soul.

With no choice left but surrender, she began to awaken to the dreamlike possibility that enlightenment was already embedded within. Noticing midlife meltdowns magically morphing into miracles, she continued pursuing a persistent premonition to play with the profound while allowing pensive purpose to gently guide her way.

Whether working through personal challenges, meeting with clients, or conducting one of her wise and witty Enlighten UP! PlayShops^{SM}, Marianne delights in looking for, and finding, the hidden shi'f't in every treasure.

She describes herself as an aspiring author, a spiritual life coach, and an eccentric senior citizen who loves nothing more than embracing the gift of eternal presence, while listening for, and following, her own Guided Omnipresent Direction within.

www.ingramcontent.com/pod-product-compliance
Lightning Source LLC
Chambersburg PA
CBHW070909130626
46555CB00001B/60